Games,
Kids, and
Christian
Education

by Susan Lennartson

Firelight

Augsburg Fortress

Contents

GAMES, KIDS,
AND CHRISTIAN EDUCATION
by Susan Lennartson

This book is dedicated to:
Olivia, the keeper of the child in the game.
Kathy, who encourages the "trail ride"
within me! *Tom*, for your unending, loving
support—as you always give! *Linda*, God
has truly blessed you with a giving spirit!
Thank you, God, for this journey! You continue to teach me in incredible ways!

Editors: Ramona Whitehurst
and Carolyn Berge
Cover: Marti Naughton
Interior design: Mike Mihelich
Photos: © 2001 PhotoDisc

Scripture quotations are from the Contemporary English Version. Copyright © 1991,
1992, 1995 American Bible Society. Used
by permission.

ISBN 0-8066-6408-8

Manufactured in the U.S.A.

05 04 03 02 01 1 2 3 4 5 6 7 8 9 10

The Game of a Lifetime

"When you are set free, you will celebrate and travel home in peace. Mountains and hills will sing as you pass by, and trees will clap." Isaiah 55:12 (CEV)

What a lively picture we draw in our minds when we read that passage of scripture. It exudes energy, calm, action and movement!

Do you remember playing as a child? I sure do. Oh, what memories. What a journey!

I was a city girl who watched the Annie Oakley TV show, and I wanted to be just like her. So, I created a horse game.

I had an imaginary horse named Chief. He was a black and white pinto that I kept in the garage of our house in a busy city neighborhood. I hooked two dog leashes together for the reins and bit. Daily, I would brush Chief, train him in jumping over picnic table benches, ride all over my neighborhood, and have some of the most incredible adventures of a lifetime.

However, one time I got in a bit of trouble. I rode Chief to school and hung the dog leashes on my locker. When someone would walk behind me, I would rear up, kick them firmly and say, "Never walk behind a horse! It's very dangerous, you know!"

My teacher firmly explained to me that I must not kick, and that I didn't have a horse. I understood the no kicking part, but the game of Chief was way too fun to do away with.

Often, other kids would play along and we would ride together. Did we have fun! I don't remember that last day that Chief and I took a ride together. The game just ended somewhere, somehow.

But what I do remember is being free to create as a child. My parents played along with the whole adventure. They saw a child of God who loved sports, running, and being active. They encouraged a very creative part of me. I remember feeling so drawn to the whole experience—the whole game. The game was life! And now, when I read Psalm 139—being fearfully and wonderfully made, knit together in my mother's womb—I think of those days of pure, unbridled fun. The days of learning what it means to be who God created me to be!

Ever say to a child, "Hey, wanna play a game?" The response will likely be, "Oh, yeah, let's go!!"

God's creation explodes with opportunities for games. God teaches us to play games through people, animals, sand, mountains, trees, ideas…and the list

> *I remember feeling so drawn to the whole experience— the whole game. The game was life!*

goes on! Learning can take place when playing a game. The invitation to play a game is often cherished at every age and in most circumstances.

Is playing a game just an escape from reality, or is a game a vital ingredient in the lives of people of all ages? Through my teaching experiences, I have found the extreme value of engaging children and adults in games to enhance a learning goal. A game adds a change of pace, can lend surprise and spontaneity.

Throughout the 1970s, I taught elementary physical education and adaptive physical education, and I coached. It was during these years that I truly learned the value of experiential learning.

During those years of teaching, I worked with Minnesota Teacher of the Year Kathryn Mumm, who was the school district's reading specialist. She had done extensive work in studying young children in the areas of reading and math. She included in the curriculum a variety of games. These games were intentionally incorporated into the journey for learning.

Some of the games involved creeping, or what we may call the Army Crawl, on a mat. Then the creeping would move to crawling. There were all sorts of fun terms used in the game. A balance beam was brought into the activity and so was a basketball.

Kathryn found that working on balance and rhythm, stimulating both sides of the body, and creatively engaging children in using their imagination, enhanced their reading and math skills.

As I began working in a church as the director of children's, family, and women's ministries, I reflected on the value of games in teaching. It led me to incorporating games in teaching the Bible. The impact was delightful!

I believe that games are the cutting edge of a learning tool in Christian education. I have experienced games to be life-giving acts of communication with God, with each other, and with our inner core.

Use this book as an igniting tool—an idea spark—a seedling of ideas. Remember that what works for one congregation may not work for another. Go through the pages, take and keep what you think might fit your learning climate.

Also, be ready to implement the new. The core of this resource is about the heart, mind, and soul of children. It's about leading them to know who Jesus is—all around them and right inside them. It's about creating a learning climate that is so exciting for children that they absolutely love coming to church and they flip over learning about God! It's about relationship and connecting.

Let's get our kids up out of their seats, looking into each other's eyes. Let's lift up their voices and hear what's in their hearts.

Once you involve games in your Christian education curriculum, whoa! Be ready! Children will be stirred with a spirit of excitement and enthusiasm. And isn't that just where our creator would have kids be! Praise God for the journey of games!

Games are the cutting edge of a learning tool in Christian education. I have experienced games to be life-giving acts of communication with God, with each other, and with our inner core.

The Case for Games in Christian Education

As Christian educators, we may ask ourselves why it is important to involve games in our curriculum. By incorporating games into our Christian education curriculum, we will impact a large mass of learners. This resource is to encourage leaders and facilitators to look at the powerful influence and impact of games in Christian education.

Games often involve several of our learning potentialities and thus enhance the learning process. Games assist in helping learners understand, comprehend, and "get it."

Where and when learners are catching the point of the session, they are automatically involved beyond merely being present—they now have become an integral part of a learning process.

Often times, we compliment ourselves in having a class of learners that sit still and listen. Well, it's true that we want to teach boundaries, expectations, values, and manners. But in teaching millennium learners, we must look to their world and our world of stimulation, change, invention and pace.

One type of experience may involve learners sitting still and looking in one direction, listening to a person speak and teach directly to them. Another experience could involve learners looking in multiple directions, getting out of their chairs, interacting with others, tasting, creating, playing games, smelling, and doing!

The use of games in Christian education invites us to a unique energy. Games ignite discussion, enhance comprehension, and help to make a learning point clearer.

Through games, we often find that the participant's involvement brings about something new, something beyond what the instructors had planned or envisioned. Games invite the unplanned. Games spark the unexpected. Games have the potential to unite us around God's message!

OBSERVE THE LEARNERS

Observe any learner learning and you will find that the learner can be totally absorbed in the play, the learning. The learner feels, plays, tries, looks, laughs, works, and is totally absorbed in the experience—the game. Great things are happening! The learner is learning through that game and then reacts to that game. The learner is making connections from the experience to life.

> *Games ignite discussion, enhance comprehension, and help to make a learning point clearer.*

Through the journey of education and learning, life connections of impact are used throughout life. Learners will rely on their senses, their intuition, and what they have learned as a guide throughout life.

Learners learn through their play. Their play is life to them. Young learners learn about God through senses and emotions. That learning process continues throughout life. Learners learn in a wide variety of ways and so, as we teach the Bible, share Scripture, and guide learners in their relationship with Christ, we must look at how we are teaching. One way does not fit everyone.

Learners respond to things that are interesting and creative. They are curious and their minds are filled with imagination. As Christian educators, we want to powerfully share the gospel with these learners. Games may help many learners understand who God is, what the Bible is about, and what it means to be a follower of Jesus.

When we say yes to teaching the Bible, teaching about who God is as our creator, and who Christ is within us, we have said yes to one of the highest calls that we will ever say yes to. In that yes, we must be forever learners in discovering creative ways to teach our learners. This is kingdom work that influences the now and impacts the future.

And so, we strive to share and teach the good news with passion—giving with energy, looking for ways to help learners understand the Bible and learn about Jesus in ways they remember for life. As we examine our lives and learning experiences, we may be able to trace important lessons we have retained. We may hold Scripture and stories in our hearts and minds due to a game or an experience that brought those life-guiding points right into our hearts.

As Christians, we have an awesome story to tell—we have some good news to proclaim. We are commissioned to go to all nations teaching and baptizing. What are we willing to give? What will we spend? How passionately will we share? What length, breadth, and height will we go to tell others about the love of Jesus?

There is a new generation being born right now. How creatively will we teach our learners? Through Christ, how will we impact the future? I believe that the future belongs to the storytellers. We are all called to passionately teach the good news to our learners so that they will grow continually in becoming living expressions of God's love.

In learning and retaining, we hope that learners will not only be able to retell biblical stories and scripture passages that they learn, but also use them as their guide and map throughout life.

Learners learn what they play and play what they learn. There is power in the use of a game and experiential learning. When learners live the Bible, they are likely to learn it. Let's not shy away from all of the fun and awesome potential of games, but rather actively embrace, incorporate, and intentionally weave games into all aspects of our Christian education process. Live it to learn it!

I have been incorporating games into our worship with learners, and training leaders to use games with our Sunday school curriculum. Here are a few of the responses and outcomes.

We must be forever learners in discovering creative ways to teach our learners. This is kingdom work that influences the now and impacts the future.

From the Learners

➤ Attendance is up—even after Christmas! Energy is up!

➤ Learners are verbalizing their ideas, thoughts, concerns, questions, joys, and suggestions. They are engaged. They are involved. They are alive.

➤ The learners are a part of teaching by their responses and investment. The learners are remembering their Bible stories as we conduct games that review what they have learned.

➤ The learners are told that they are important ministers.

➤ Learning about God is fun!

➤ "I love to be at church," they say.

From the Families

➤ Parents are ignited because their learners are ignited.

➤ Through a take-home newsletter and congregation devotion booklet, parents are trying the learning games in their homes. Now, we have home as church too.

From the Leaders

➤ One leader said, "I love our curriculum. You make teaching so easy!"

➤ Another said, "This was an awesome session. My only regret is that even more children were not here to experience it."

➤ Leaders are trained and equipped with creative teaching games.

➤ The leaders are having a positive experience. They will come back and they will encourage others to teach.

➤ Leaders feel as though they are helping learners to see and experience God's love and direction for them through the games. They sense that they are making a difference in the lives of learners.

Christian education will be changed forever through the use of games. Through a Bible learning game, learners will be transformed forever!

*Learning
about God
is fun!*

Chapter 2

The Power, Passion, and Journey of Games

THE POWER OF GAMES

I spoke with a man who had attended a training retreat on team building, communication, and leadership development. His large corporation felt that it was absolutely necessary for everyone in the company to attend a training that involved games of challenge, team building, and process work.

Not everyone could go at the same time, so, over a couple of years, teams of people were sent to an out-of-state location to partake in team-building games of challenge. The games involved problem solving, adventure, risk taking, cooperation, competition, self-discovery, fun, and dialog for learning.

The man said that the games involved several learning styles in one activity. He felt that the games moved people into an incredible time of discussion. The real learning happened when the team wholeheartedly got into the game and spent time talking about how it related to their work in the company.

The company benefited strongly by investing in the training. The games helped to identify leaders. They help to discover skills, desires, talents, and passions. The team members realized that the games were completed only through teamwork. They saw that there were times when someone drops the ball, or falls from a rope, or takes a wrong turn. They took the experience of the game and transferred the sessions into their life journeys.

This is a fantastic way to learn. For some, it is not easy or even comfortable to take part in a game. For some, it is awesome and they become energized by it. But for everyone, there is something to learn and much to retain!

Games involve problem solving, adventure, risk taking, cooperation, competition, self-discovery, fun, and dialog for learning.

THE PASSION OF THE GAME—HOW JESUS TAUGHT

Have you ever studied the way Jesus taught? He often taught using parables, short stories told to teach a session by directly involving those around him. He used experiential learning to leave an imprint of strong influence. Experiential learning is learning by and through and experience in which we engage our learning modalities.

For an example, let's journey back to Maundy Thursday.

That night, Jesus took bread, gave it to his disciples and said, "Take this. This is my body which is broken for you." He also took a cup of wine and said, "Drink this. This is my blood which is shed for you." Also on that night, he took a cloth from around him and a basin of water, knelt before the feet of his disciples, held their feet tenderly, looked into their eyes, and washed their feet.

Peter responded by saying, "Jesus, you should not wash my feet. I should wash your feet." Jesus said, "No, Peter. I want you to experience this. Remember this—I want you to serve others as I have served you. I came into the world, not to be served, but to serve." At that, Peter said, "Then wash all of me, Jesus." Jesus responded by saying, "No, just the feet, Peter!"

Those words, that act, that experience was one of the most important lessons that Jesus taught. The impact of that experience influences us today. If we want to know the heart of Christ, we will be on our knees, living as biblical servants, striving to be biblically generous.

I also love the story about Jesus raising Lazarus from the dead. I'm sure that it was quite an experience for everyone witnessing that miracle. Upon the stone being rolled away from the tomb, Lazarus was called by name. He rose and stood before everyone. Lazarus had been in the tomb for four days, wrapped and oiled. The sight, no doubt, was amazing.

Jesus could have said, "Clothes be gone," and immediately the clothes binding Lazarus would have left him. But instead, Jesus called out to the group to unbind him. Again, Jesus invited a community of people into an experience. It had to have been smelly, difficult, and possibly frightening, as well as unbelievable—but Jesus calls us to do the difficult and the uneasy. Again, Jesus taught through an experience of senses and emotion.

What a model Jesus is for us in education. He taught with simplicity, emotion, experiences, stories, metaphors, visuals.

OUR LIFE JOURNEY OF LEARNING

All across the world we hear of organizations, corporations, schools, and congregations that are teaching and training using a wide variety of games. We continue to learn more and more about multiple intelligences, learning potentials, and emotional intelligence.

Colleges and universities send students out to experience teaching—an experience known as student teaching—as part of their college course requirement. Doctors and pastors experience an internship of experience as an integral part of their learning.

The Montessori model of teaching is based on experiential learning. The model of "workshop rotation" in Christian education involves games of experiential learning. When we involve several of our senses in learning experiences, retention is high and impact is strong.

My Personal Journey

For several years, I have been traveling across the United States, meeting with a wide variety of congregations. They are all very unique, very different, and yet all one—we worship one God. My focus has been in the areas of children's family ministry, women's ministry, and volunteer ministry.

Those are very broad areas, ones that are deeply seated in church. They are areas of ministry that involve every aspect of discipleship. Every workshop, semi-

When we involve several of our senses in learning experiences, retention is high and impact is strong.

nar, and keynote address that I give embraces the vital message of active learning—the use of games and experiential learning in Christian education today. I not only talk about it, but participants also live out the learning.

Throughout my growing and years of seasoning, my learning has been impacted by what I call "Games of Ah-Ha." Leaders have led me through a most profound learning experience where something clicked and I got it—I caught and grasped the idea, the thought, the lesson, and the way! This has been a whole life journey of learning for me. I am always struck by how we learn through a game and play situation.

As a young mother, I remember observing my son Eric. He was a Lego master at an early age. He rarely followed the exact instructions in constructing the Lego project. He created as he played. Eric loved building, design, and creative shapes. As a young boy he designed an elementary school, and before he made a tree fort, he would draw out the plans. Our hills for sliding in the winter were a work of art as Eric designed curves, bridges, and mazes in the snow.

There were many gifts brewing in Eric's play. I watched, encouraged, and empowered my son as well as provided an arena of freedom for expression. Today, as an adult, Eric is a creative architect and artist. God blessed him with unique gifts. Throughout his life, he has experientially lived out who and what God has so masterfully created him to be.

My life journey of being in tune to and drawn to experiential learning situations is an absolute gift from God. It draws me to help and teach those with special needs because I know that they will prosper through the use of games. And it calls me to teach and spark in those who are sharing the gospel, proclaiming Christ and telling the good news.

There is an amazingly exciting way to format Christian education. It is through implementing games and experiences into our curriculum. This learning style is filled with an incredible journey. It's about fun, about being bold, about impact—and it's for the now!

God has blessed me with a passion for teaching the gospel through games and experiential learning. God has blessed me with energy and enthusiasm to share, to give away. Jesus reminds me:

➢ to be aware of people of all ages and stages and how they learn.

➢ to be available to travel, speak, write, teach, and share what God has taught me.

➢ to be accepting of change, challenge, and the cost of discipleship.

➢ to abide in God's way.

➢ and to abandon the things that I must in order to be obedient to where God calls me to journey.

When we use our gifts to glorify God—wow, what a journey! When we strive to be obedient to where God leads us—wow, what an experience. I have watched, I have heard, I have felt, I have experienced, and I continue to grow in learning more and more about the impact and influence of games and active learning in Christian education. I have no doubt that it is one of the strongest tools in teaching the future generations the good news!

The Passion in the Journey

Life is a journey in which we see, hear, smell, and taste a smorgasbord of learning situations. As we go about this journey, it takes passion and commitment to know purpose. On that journey we are forever learners that are constantly being shaped and molded. Here are some journeys in which I have found that games have shaped attitudes, memories, and feelings have been conceptualized.

Journey #1

I received a wonderful gift one early December. It was a small book with an accompanying CD based on the song "Mary, Did You Know?" by Buddy Greene and Mark Lowry. My friend who blessed me with this gift told me that the song came alive to her through a most tender experience. Her preschool daughter, in hearing the song, wanted to "live" the song, and so she created a game.

The child draped fabric over her head, wrapped a doll in cloth, and cradled this doll in her arms as she listened to the music. She rocked back and forth, nestled in the stairway, caressing the baby and tenderly kissing it. With a free, childlike heart and mind, the girl experienced the message of that song through a game that was spontaneously created by her. Through her senses, emotions, and spontaneity, a game was birthed.

My friend, with tears in her eyes, pictured the young mother of Jesus, Mary, holding Christ. Did Mary know that as she kissed her little baby, she kissed the face of God? Oh, Mary, did you know?

Journey #2

I remember my son Ryan absolutely loving a particular children's book series about a boy and his dog who went on awesome adventures together. We would read the story over and over! Ryan, in his own childlike, creative, and imaginary way would then live out the book through a game that he created.

He would pack his backpack, make marking flags with the letter R for Ryan, draw pictures of his adventure, map out his journey, prepare food, and then announce to me that he would be going on an adventure.

It was all so real and serious to him. Our dog was a part of the journey as well. There was fun in the learning as Ryan truly lived this story. His style of learning and his joy in the game remains a precious memory for me.

As I watched Ryan, I remember wondering, God, what adventures do you have in store for my son as he travels through life? Raise him up on eagle's wings. Lord!

Journey #3

As an adult, I was part of a leadership training workshop to prepare a college ministry team for its mission trip to Jamaica. About one-third of the way into our training, we played a game.

Everyone in the group (there were about 40 of us) was given a piece of paper with a number on it. We were to look at the number, not show it to anyone,

As we go about this journey, it takes passion and commitment to know purpose.

memorize it, and then put it in our pocket. Next, we stood up and formed a circle. Then, we were given a cloth to put over our eyes and told not to speak.

As all these preliminary instructions and rules were given, we were told that our mission was to find the other person in the group with the same number as ours. All numbers were in pairs. We were to do this without using our eyes or words.

However, we had other means and resources and it was up to us to discover a way to use our resources in finding our matching number. The game began. It was an amazing journey.

We discovered that we could use our legs to walk and move, our hands to clap out our number, our feet to stomp the number, our fingers to draw out the number in another's palm or on their back, and on and on. Through this game, we were challenged to complete the mission. It was fun, difficult, and challenging, and filled with action, creativity, surprises, and accomplishment. We all found our matching numbers!

On completing the game, we moved into a discussion and process time. We shared that, at the beginning of the game, the goal of finding the matching numbers sounded impossible. We also discussed the importance of communication as a team.

The game brought out a lot of dialog. We completed our process time by talking about how God communicates with us and how we communicate with God.

We also talked about how God supplies us with all the resources that we need. Our guiding Bible verse was, "I will be with you always, even until the end of the world" (Matthew 28:20 CEV). Even though parts of the mission trip seemed impossible, we grew through our discussion in knowing that through Christ, all things are possible!

The experience of this and other Games of Ah-Ha have stayed with me for years.

Journey #4

As a child growing up in an urban congregation, I was a faithful, weekly Sunday school and summer vacation Bible school attendee. Whenever and wherever a leader provided a situation where the class could "live" a Bible session through a game or experiential learning, I learned in a most energized way. The point of the story and session being taught stuck with me in a whole new way.

One of my teachers had us move and dance to the song "This Is My Father's World." We were studying creation. I sing that song now and feel the movement of God's creation within me.

The game brought out a lot of dialog. We completed our process time by talking about how God communicates with us and how we communicate with God.

On Your Mark! Get Set for the Game!

Chapter 3

You're at the starting line, in the blocks—ready for the race to begin. You crouch down, get your hands and feet in place. Your hips are raised into the starting position. Your mind is already racing, and you're focused on what you need to do. Then, the buzzer sounds and you passionately go for the finish line!

But, before you stood in the starting blocks, you spent a good amount of time in preparation and training to run the race. There were others along the way who helped coach and encourage you. You worked hard because you had a passion and desire to do well.

You're now equipped for the race with just the right shoes, you're wearing a uniform for comfort and identity, and maybe you have a sweat band around your head so that those drops of sweat won't block your vision. You're ready, you're set, you're on the mark, and you're excited to go!

A similar process will take place in preparing to implement games into your Christian education curriculum. Let's walk through those steps.

It's important to develop a frame of teamwork.

"GETTING STARTED" STEPS

1. The Vision

Do you or does someone have a desire to integrate games into your Christian education style of teaching? Do you believe that learning through a game format has value in Christian education? Do you have a passion for making Scripture stick?

There needs to be someone—or a group of people—who shares an excitement for the power and value of using games in teaching the Bible. Find them.

It is not critical that you know everything there is to know about games. You don't even need to begin at this point with mountains of experience in teaching games. The know-how and the experience will come. What you do need is someone who is enthusiastic about this journey. Are you there?

Meet with your church staff, children's ministries staff, or children's ministries volunteer Team to discuss the importance and implementation of games in Christian education. It's important to develop a frame of teamwork.

2. Getting Equipped

Take training and equipping very seriously. We want leaders who are prepared and feel comfortable with what they are called to do as they move ahead.

Learners deserve energized, equipped leaders. Give leaders the important tools necessary in teaching games. Build people for success.

Spend time in reviewing resources and curriculum. Work at becoming well informed about the material. Collaborate as a team to decide what games will be used, what ages will be taught, what space will be available, and what supplies will be needed.

People as Coaches and Resources

Talk to people who teach games and use games as teaching tools. They will be an important resource and may assist with training.

These resources may include people that:

➢ work at a camp teaching learners through games. People in outdoor ministry know and value the impact of experiential learning through games.

➢ teach elementary physical education. They know deeply how to teach through the physical.

➢ train in the corporate world. Oftentimes trainers have wonderful games that they use to bring a learning point into focus.

➢ work at the YMCA or YWCA. Ask if there is a games specialist on staff.

➢ teach learners at school or in sports.

I have found these people to be wonderful resources. They know how games can teach. They also know how to teach a game directly and clearly. Connect with these resources in your congregation and community for assistance in equipping you and your staff.

3. Equipment and Space

Now that you are trained, prepare the playing area. What props or supplies are needed? Is the space available going to work? You want to know the game and how to do it, and be ready with supplies. It helps to do a practice run of the game—in the space where the game will be taught, with props in place.

4. Go for It

You're ready—GO! Play the game. Enjoy the process. Rely on your training to facilitate and teach with confidence. Be a leader.

5. Dialog, Discussion, Process Time

Have a process in place for evaluations. Think ahead. Review what was taught. Ask for feedback on the use of games in your Christian education curriculum. Get input from adults as well as children.

Remember—integrating an aggressive, passionate format of games into your Christian education curriculum may feel like eating an elephant in one big bite. It's hard to do—so take one little bite at a time!

Learning through Games

Chapter 4

I often lead family retreats. On one particular "Dads and Daughters" retreat, we implemented a ropes course activity. The challenge was for each person to get up on a cable, approximately six feet off the ground, that was stretched between two strong trees.

The game was this: One person at a time started at one end of the cable and attempted to side-step all the way to the other end. For stabilization, there was a lead rope—pencil thin—to hold on to, if desired. That cable would begin to wave back and forth, making it very difficult to stay up on it. The lead rope helped somewhat.

I was warned not to wrap the lead rope around my hand, because when I fell, the rope could tear my hand. For total safety, the person on the cable would be "spotted" on both sides by people on the ground. Any group using the ropes course had to be trained to do this.

Well, my turn was up! There I was—up about six feet off the ground, about to launch my journey from one end of the cable to the other. I made it about one-quarter of the way, then the cable started to wobble back and forth. I held tightly to the lead rope, thinking I could pull myself to stability.

I looked down and saw all of the dads and daughters, their hands in the air, ready to catch me in their arms. (I'm sure they were thinking, "I sure hope she falls the other way!") Well, fall I did, and into their arms I landed—safe and secure.

When the game was over, we all gathered to talk about the game. Through our discussion, I learned that oftentimes as a leader, I am the one doing the catching, the saving, the holding, and the spotting for multiple people and programs.

Now I was on the rope. I was reminded that, as a leader, there are loving people all around me to help and catch me when I fall. I was reminded that God's loving arms are there for me continually.

Leading all of us through the game was an insightful leader who took us on a journey of learning. The trained leader carefully walked us through the vital steps in teaching the game and then in processing the game. These steps are so important—they are what makes the game a teaching tool.

Following are four important steps in leading and teaching games in Christian education. In using games to teach the Bible, the process goes way beyond the game itself—it becomes a learning journey of the mind, heart, soul, and life. This process calls for a perceptive, well-prepared leader who is in tune and able to capture teachable moments.

Oftentimes as a leader, I am the one doing the catching, the saving, the holding, and the spotting for multiple people and programs.

It is important for a leader to know these four steps. They form the process of guiding a group learning experience through games. Please walk through the steps so we can be on the same page as we think through this learning journey.

The steps are:

1. The game is taught. (Giving direction for the activity)

2. The game is played. (The adventure and journey of the game)

3. The game is discussed to reveal the learning points. (Debriefing and learning valuable lessons)

4. The learning points of the game are used in everyday life. (Life links to God's Word that we hope will stick for life)

Now, let's dig into this journey and the whole process of teaching games.

STEPS IN LEADING AND TEACHING GAMES IN CHRISTIAN EDUCATION

Step #1
Journey of the Mind—The Game Is Taught

As we introduce a game to a group of learners, first draw a mind picture. We invite the learners to visualize what they are about to experience. As we give directions for the game, learners will start to conceptualize how it will be played out.

It is helpful during directions to demonstrate the game. It would be boring if we just read the instructions. Keep fun and creativity in mind when teaching the game. Speak clearly and use visuals with the explanation. Ask for questions to make sure that everyone is clear as to what they are about to be engaged in. Stir the imagination with enthusiasm and excitement.

Expect learners to listen, and do not move ahead unless you know that everyone has been attentive. It is beneficial to have someone model the activity before the game begins. Do all that you can within this time to help learners visualize what they are about to do. This is a vital step due to its strong impact on safety.

Think about the following steps for #1:

➤ Describe the game.

➤ Demonstrate it.

➤ Ask if there are any questions.

➤ Prepare for the game.

➤ Expect attentiveness.

➤ Do not move ahead unless you feel that learners understand your directions, rules, and boundaries.

➤ Don't let this time of teaching the game get too drawn out—you'll lose the group. Keep it moving.

➤ Make sure that everyone knows the rules, safety concerns, their part in the game, and how the game is played.

It is helpful during directions to demonstrate the game. It would be boring if we just read the instructions.

Step #2
Journey of the Heart—The Game Is Played

This part is the actual entrance point of being physically and emotionally involved in the game itself. The heart and whole being of the learner is involved. Participants will be following directions, playing out the game, cooperating or competing, and learning as they are engaged in, with, and through the journey of a game.

There may be an element of surprise that happens as the game is played. What a learner pictured the game to be and what the learner actually experiences in the game, may not be exactly the same. Learners' feelings, emotions, and senses are highly involved during this process. The participants will be engaged with the very core of activity.

It may be necessary for a leader at some point to stop the game and repeat or reframe the teaching points of the game. The game may not be going in the direction that the leader feels is safe or productive. Be ready to adapt, if needed.

Or the game may be stopped so that the leader may bring out an important learning moment. A perceptive leader sees where interrupting the game to add insight, challenge, or encouragement may be a vital step for enhancing the quality of the learning experience.

And it is important to know when to stop the game while everyone is still having a good time. Don't overplay a game to the point of learners becoming tired or bored with it.

We hope that all learners involved with a game will:
- ➢ have a sense of belonging.
- ➢ have an opportunity to participate.
- ➢ feel safe.
- ➢ be given choices.
- ➢ feel respected and valued.
- ➢ get their whole being—body and brain—involved.
- ➢ have a lot of fun.

This is such an important step in the learning process. Learners play games at home, at school, and in their neighborhoods. Now, we as Christian educators have an opportunity to invite learners to a game that takes place at church. How will it be unique and different?

What will they remember from this experience? Will it be a positive, fun memory or will there be a fearful negative image left in their hearts and minds? We are leader-dependent!

We have a learner in our hands. Teaching games calls for an insightful leader, ready and able to direct a group of learners through a safe, fun, engaging, Christ-centered experience.

Remember, as you are doing the activity—playing the game—be ready to adapt, change, or add a new twist! You are the leader.

At some point, stop the game and repeat or reframe the teaching points of the game.

Step #3
The Journey of Process—Talk about the Game

Upon finishing and completing the game, it is time to process what the learners have just experienced. During this unique time of creative processing, the game becomes an experience of "ah-ha."

The objective of the learning is now transformed, we hope, into the mind to form a connection—a life link—between mind, heart, and soul. We hope that learners will comprehend the connection of the game to the goal of the session being taught.

The leader will serve as a teacher as well as a facilitator during this process time. A creative and clear process time following a game experience can answer "Why did we play this game?" It is a time to examine the core of the game experience.

As well as having fun playing the game, our goal is to move into a teachable moment. Guide learners into a creative discussion of why and how the game relates to the Bible.

As leaders, we must always be mindful of age appropriateness. Pace, age, maturity, place, length of time, and objectives to be taught are important considerations as we plan for games in Christian education curriculum. It is natural to think that the younger the learner, the shorter the process time allowed and, thus, the older the learner, the longer we may be involved in process.

Generally, this conclusion stands true, but I believe we will be in for some great surprises as we:

➤ involve more creative, educational games into our teaching style and Christian education curriculum.

➤ watch those learners respond and open up with incredible thoughts through their simple way of seeing things. They are profound.

➤ invite and encourage learners to respond in a directed yet free, creative process time, even with our young learners.

➤ take great care with our process time to draw out all ideas and thoughts from learners. Respect all ideas and thoughts, even if they have absolutely nothing to do with the session theme.

➤ affirm the learner's input during the process time.

➤ ask for and expect new insight into the game objective from learners. Invite their ideas. What did they see, feel, or experience through the game that had not been discussed?

➤ carefully and creatively train leaders and facilitators to lead learners through the journey of games and process time.

➤ are reminded that we are leader-dependent. A good, insightful leader will draw out insights and wisdom from the learners. To educate, we are called to draw ideas out, not stuff them in.

➤ remember that learning is a journey.

It's also important to remember that the leader moves into a critical facilitator role during this process. Be careful not to do all of the "mind work" for the

As leaders, we must always be mindful of:
- *age appropriateness*
- *pace*
- *age*
- *maturity*
- *place*
- *length of time*
- *objectives*

learners. Allow them the journey of working at finding the reason and Bible-life link of the game. Ask questions and guide the discussion. Allow the learners the opportunity to work.

Step #4
The Journey of Life Application

This is an amazing area of learning. We may or may not see the fruits of this "life link" learning, but we hope the lessons learned will be retained and used any time during a lifetime. We never know when we will recall the message of what we have learned through a game.

Through my personal experience, I find that whenever I have lived a game and processed its meaning, I am likely to use, apply, and transform the information into a wide variety of situations and decisions. For a large mass of learners, an active learning experience has high impact and strong retention.

Games help us to recall the objective of the lesson because we have heard it, played it, talked about it, saw it, felt it—maybe even tasted it or smelled it. We want lessons from the Bible to stick. Games serve as a part of the educational adhesives in bringing God's message right into our very being.

This step of learning moves into our knowing—our comprehension. Did we really grasp the message?

Where might the impact of our game learning experiences be transformed? I believe that what we learn through living a lesson may affect how we:

➢ solve problems throughout life.
➢ make decisions on a daily basis.
➢ seek to create and shape our environment and how we live as disciples.
➢ sustain and renew our growth and well-being as a Christian.
➢ grow in relationship and understanding of God, our creator.
➢ journey through life as a follower of Jesus.
➢ live to know who we are, in and through Christ.
➢ stand firm in our commitment to Christian values.
➢ travel as Advent people on a Lenten journey with Easter vision.
➢ become biblically generous as biblical servants.

Learners are living, breathing works of art, playing out the game of life. Our learners must be played with, talked to, sung to, read to, interacted with, held, loved, and touched with the care of Christ. Learners are God's tapestry of love. They, like we, are an unfinished tapestry. You are a weaver; weave with vibrancy!

To set the stage in learning through games, it is important for us to value the process. We must not only see the process of games in education, but truly value, with passion, the impact and the holistic value of each stage—each step, in learning through games.

May all Christian educators invite learners into a journey of feeling, reflecting, thinking, doing, analyzing, playing, and sharing. Through a game experience, God can open a world of lasting wisdom!

Learners are living, breathing works of art, playing out the game of life. Our learners must be played with, talked to, sung to, read to, interacted with, held, loved, and touched with the care of Christ. Learners are God's tapestry of love.

Chapter 5

Games to Teach Leaders

Leaders are very important for the implementation of games in Christian education. They have a strong effect on the overall quality of the experience.

I have found that whenever I use games in our training sessions, through participating in a game experience, a leader will see, feel, and sense, wholeheartedly, the impact of games.

First of all, I call all of our training sessions "Igniter Meetings." That's what we must be about in our equipping and training sessions—the experience must be sandwiched with excitement and enthusiasm.

Following are a few games that I have used in helping leaders experience the benefits of games in education. It shows ways for the leaders to sense and feel the learning power of a game.

HAND AND ARM FOLDING

I have used this game many times with a leader training session. It's fun for leaders to use this game with their classes:

Fold hands as in prayer. Turn to the person next to you. Which thumb is on top? The right or the left? Unfold your hands and refold them with the opposite thumb on top. How does it feel? Odd, uncomfortable, unnatural? Now, fold your arms. Turn to the person next to you. Which arm is on the top? The right or the left? Now, unfold your arms. Then refold them with the opposite arm on top. How does it feel?

Wow—I can hardly do it. My arms keep falling out of place. (You—yes, you, the one reading this resource—try this exercise now. Put the book down now!)

This is an exercise in change. How does change feel? Different, uncomfortable, unnatural, unique, odd, or funny? But, we tried it and we did it! We took something that we always do—in fact, we do it naturally—without giving it a lot of thought, like folding our hands and arms—and we tried doing these natural things in a different way.

How may we relate this to our lives, our congregations, our world? In lay ministry, in life, what are some changes we may encounter?

At this point, we take time to talk about change. I find that in many congregations change is a constant. It's not always easy, but God is with us in all of the changes.

Also, we may talk about who we are, most naturally. When we naturally fold our hands and arms, there is a way that feels comfortable and natural.

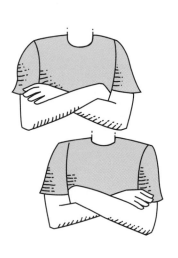

Hand and Arm Folding

When are we our most natural selves? What situations or settings take place where we feel very comfortable and natural? How does who we are and how we are created affect our ministry roles? How has God created you? Are you fully aware of your giftedness?

We didn't try crossing our legs. But let's. Try crossing your legs both ways. Does one way feel more natural than the other way? Is it comfortable both ways?

What are the things in life that we do where we can be flexible and comfortable in a variety of situations? Relate this experience to volunteering in a church. Relate this to being a Sunday school leader.

How does all this relate to teaching Sunday school? What changes are we experiencing in Sunday school today? How are learners changing? How was Saul changed in the Bible? Finally, how will God change our lives as we follow his guidance?

O'METER WARM-UP

Use your hands and arms to be a meter with a 0 to 10 gauge. Stretch your left arm to the side—that will be the O (least) marking on the meter. Draw your right arm—the needle on the meter—across from 0 to 10 (right arm fully extended to the right side). Bring the needle (your right arm) to the 3 area on the meter. Ask the group what clapping sounds like at a 3. Move the needle to different positions, and have the group try clapping at a 5, and next at a 10. You've created the Clap O' Meter.

O'Meter Warm-Up

Also try a Yeah O' Meter, Stomp O' Meter, Amen O' Meter, or Praise God O' Meter. Give it all at 10!

Discuss how everyone worked together to achieve a specific sound at each level, and how each level was great. Everyone got their hands moving and voices warmed up!

Ask what a team sounds like when they work together. What does it feel like to work as a team? I wonder what it would have been like to be a disciple? Probably a "10," since disciples got to listen and learn at the feet of the Master. How do we work together as a team?

How does Jesus want us to behave as a team? How is your Sunday school or children's ministries team working together? Staff as well as volunteers are all part of the ministry team. Are your hands serving God? Are your voices praising the Lord?

BALLOON PRAYER

(Be sure to check for latex allergies before beginning this activity.)

Give each leader a balloon. I use good-sized, good-quality, beautifully colored balloons. Have each person blow up his or her balloon, tie a knot in it, and then hold it up to carefully admire its color, shape, size, and luminosity.

Hold up a balloon that has not been blown up. Point out its characteristics: It is flat, limp, and opaque. Dense in color and boring. What can you do with it in this state?

Then say, "Look at your balloon again. It is changed because you have breathed life into it. It is not the same because you have given it a part of yourself through that burst of air. You gave it the very thing that keeps you alive!"

Emphasize how the color has changed. Blown up, the balloon is bright, light, and luminous. It can be used in many ways to bring joy and delight to others—which is exactly what God has done for all of us. We are changed by the presence of the Holy Spirit within us. As Paul exuberantly states in Philippians 4:13, "Christ gives me the strength to face anything."

Leaders give of themselves to their learners and the learners' lives are changed because of it. Like a cheerful balloon, a leader gives newness to a learner.

Ask the leaders to once again study their balloons. This time, they should picture a learner they'd like to pray for. Say, "You have a learner in your hands. Who is that learner? Pray for that learner now. Think about that learner as a treasure to God." After a while, pray out loud for all the learners represented.

Oftentimes after our prayer time, I encourage our leaders to turn to the person next to them and share who they prayed for and perhaps why they prayed for that learner.

Balloon Prayer

Balloon Launch

To close, launch the balloons. Say: "As we lifted all of these leaders up in prayer, let's lift up all these balloons in prayer. Peter Benson has a book titled *All Kids Are Our Kids*—and now, all balloons are our balloons! Let's keep every one of them up in the air as we focus on all of God's kids the balloons represent. Let's lift them all up in prayer and support!"

Turn on some music to play as the group works to keep all the balloons aloft. It's a beautiful visual, and the laughter and energy in the room is fabulous.

Afterward, talk about how leaders are a team in lifting up each learner and in raising them all up as disciples. God is always with us, to lift us up and to keep us aloft. I have found that this game really touches hearts as we think about our precious learners and how we seek to shepherd their hearts.

As the game comes to a close and all of the balloons settle, I invite the leaders to join me in another journey: listening to the story of Zacchaeus.

The Story of Zacchaeus

Ask the leaders to think about the balloon activity as you read the story.

Jesus was walking through Jericho. He was busy. There were crowds all around wanting to see him and he was on his way—as we now know—to the cross. Zacchaeus wanted to see Jesus, as everyone did. However, Zacchaeus was elbowed out from a frontline curbside view. Zacchaeus was not the most popular person in town. And so he climbed a tree and eagerly waited for Jesus to pass by.

When Jesus did come by, he stopped, looked up in the tree and said to Zacchaeus, "Come on down, Zacchaeus. I'm coming to your house today." That encounter changed Zacchaeus's life!

Usually, the story of Zacchaeus focuses on the wee little man up in a sycamore tree. But now, focus instead on what Jesus did for Zacchaeus that day. Ask, "What can we learn about what Jesus wants us to be about? How does this story impact us as Sunday school leaders?"

Here is what Jesus did. First, he was aware of the one up in the tree. Are we aware of those learners in our classes that are "hangin' up in the tree?" Who are they? How can we grow to become more like Jesus and see with our heart those who are longing to belong?

Next, Jesus was available. He was busy, he had a lot to do, but he stopped and gave of his time to be with one who needed him. Say, "As a Sunday school leader, you are giving of your time. You are saying to learners, 'I'm here for you. I give you my time and my care. I'm available to teach you about God.'"

Jesus was accepting. He could have had a meal with the most prestigious people in town, but he chose to go to the home of Zacchaeus. Jesus accepted Zacchaeus, even though the townspeople disliked him.

As a chief tax collector, Zacchaeus was at odds with the people. How accepting are we to those around us—the learners, their families, those with whom we are in ministry? May we grow to follow the example of Jesus and be open with a heart of acceptance.

Ask the leaders to again think about that balloon. Remind them that they put into the balloon the very thing that gives them life. When leaders are aware, available, and accepting toward learners, they fill learners' lives in a new way. Through the power of the Holy Spirit, learners will be changed.

If we incorporate games into our teaching of adults, they will learn in a new way because they have lived it. If we want our Sunday school to be exciting, then we must make our leader meetings beyond exciting. They must be like a retreat whereby leaders feel renewed, revived, ignited, and excited to tell kids about Jesus. Just watch how a game of "ah-ha" ignites your equipping time!

Chapter 6

How Do Learners Develop?

Many of you work with preschool through sixth grade learners. You are also working in family ministry. The following are descriptions of how learners develop. Consider these when making your game choices.

PRESCHOOLERS

What an incredible crew. Their energy would heat the world! As you incorporate games into their Christian education experience, remember that preschoolers:

➤ look to God as the creator of trees, birds, worms. and watermelon!
➤ love to be active and moving.
➤ live on their creative imaginations.
➤ are learning their alphabet, colors, and shapes.
➤ need help in forming a circle or gathering in a line.
➤ have an attention span that is short, but grows as they grow.
➤ learn through the senses and emotion.
➤ may be unsure about not being with mom or dad.
➤ can hop, jump, run, crawl, and dance freely
➤ are advancing in balance.
➤ need to feel safe.
➤ love to have fun.
➤ need to be loved.
➤ like to be chosen; like attention.
➤ clearly display their emotions and feelings.
➤ view play as their work.
➤ often play what they see—they are imitators.
➤ like songs with action.
➤ find large-muscle activities easier than small-muscle activities.
➤ often move freely and spontaneously to music.
➤ like to help each other.
➤ love their teachers and leaders.
➤ learn about God by coming to his house, the church.
➤ learn about God through people showing God's love and care for them.
➤ respond to echo prayers.
➤ are distracted easily.

Preschoolers learn about God through people showing God's love and care for them.

KINDERGARTNERS TO THIRD GRADERS

There is a lot of growth that takes place between kindergarten and third grade. Watch the children as they move through these years. I truly enjoy being with this age group. I don't think that I will ever tire of praising God and playing a game with young children this age!

They:

- are inquisitive.
- love games.
- love stories.
- are learning a lot.
- need help and direction in taking a rest or pause with their busy energy.
- learn through active learning experiences.
- believe that God loves them.
- look to God as the creator of the earth.
- know Jesus as God's Son and feel sorry for Jesus dying on the cross.
- need to feel safe.
- like to have fun.
- need to feel loved and wanted.
- have reading skills that are growing.
- still ask a lot of "why"" questions.
- enjoy their teachers and leaders.
- develop friends.
- have a beautiful Christ-like faith.
- can listen and follow rules.
- can start praying on their own.
- think about heaven ("My pet is in heaven with God.")
- learn very well through games.
- are learning how to read very well.
- are learning to tell time.
- are learning how to write cursive.
- are becoming more coordinated.
- understand teams.
- love their friends.
- enjoy Bible stories.
- pray to God.
- are growing physically at a rapid rate.
- love to move rather than sit.
- are sensitive.
- can function in a large-group game.
- have great ideas to share.

Learners in kindergarten through third grade know Jesus as God's Son and feel sorry for Jesus dying on the cross.

FOURTH TO SIXTH GRADERS

This age is a pre-teen age. They are wonderful conversationalists. I have found their wisdom and discernment to be incredible. They are growing at a very fast pace, stepping up to the doorstep of the teen years. When I'm at camp with this age group, I enjoy just hanging out with them. They are at an awesome stage in life.

They:

➤ want to be about the "now," and yet are able to think futuristically.
➤ love God and Jesus, and are growing to understand the Holy Spirit.
➤ need to feel loved and wanted.
➤ love to have fun.
➤ need to feel safe.
➤ are making decisions and choices.
➤ are growing in their reading skills.
➤ are discovering their leadership skills.
➤ can sit and process.
➤ can pair-share.
➤ want to be exposed to any movie, song, Web site, video, or experience.
➤ need strong parental guidance.
➤ love games.
➤ understand teams.
➤ love to be physical.
➤ can play hard and still need direction in pausing for times of rest.
➤ are becoming very social.
➤ believe friends are very important.
➤ know their likes and dislikes.
➤ (many of them) can pray freely.
➤ can relate the Old Testament to New Testament stories when presented.
➤ are growing to comprehend Holy Communion.
➤ want to do what's right and good.
➤ are growing regarding their questions about God.
➤ may begin to take music lessons.
➤ are identifying what they like to do and who they want to be with.
➤ often have very busy schedules—already!
➤ might feel a need to act "cool."
➤ are changing physically at a very measurable rate.
➤ might catch "junior high-" or "middle school-itis."
➤ may test authority a bit more than when they were younger.

All learners are so very unique and different and mature at a wide variety of rates. Environment, homes, school, and church affect their growth. People in their lives impact their decisions and identity.

What learners are exposed to and what they experience often affects their outlook on life. God has created them with gifts and talents and, thus, it is a joy

> *Learners in fourth to sixth grade love God and Jesus, and are growing to understand the Holy Spirit.*

to observe the developmental steps they progress through. Learners need to be nurtured and looked upon with great value. We must picture a great future for each learner and then take an active role in helping that future come to be.

Always be aware of where learners are in their emotional, social, and physical development stages. As you plan games and design learning experiences, remember that the heart of a learner is being impacted. Strive to know your learner in and out!

And—one last important thought. Is someone in your Sunday school praying for each learner by name? Do not assume this is taking place. As we look to involve the whole learner in a game experience so that they will grow to learn God's Word, let's also make sure that the total learner is being prayed for by name! You are holding a learner in your arms. Treasure and bless each precious one.

Chapter 7

Igniter Sparks to Start

We sing in a popular Christian song that it only takes one spark to get a fire burning. Here are some sparks to help launch you into the implementation of games for your Christian education curriculum. Actually, I hope that these igniter thoughts and ideas serve as a blow torch to get you really fired up for games! But, before we get into some of the game spark ideas, let's take a look at what it takes to keep the fire burning.

THE FIRE

To make a campfire, you need:
1. A match or a spark—to ignite it
2. Kindling, paper, wood—to fuel it
3. Oxygen—to keep it alive

Here are three areas of focus that will help keep your fire for games ablaze and filled with energy.

Focus #1
The Leader-Facilitator-Coach

This role is vital. The leader must explain the game, the rules, the safety precautions, the whole game process and the motivation of the game. This person, and his or her leadership, is key.

This leader is a person that:

➢ is enthusiastic about the use of games in Christian education and has a contagious Christian spirit.

➢ is able to clearly and understandably give directions for the game.

➢ understands positive and direct boundaries for the physical and emotional safety of all learners.

➢ values being prepared.

➢ is familiar with learning characteristics of the learners being taught.

➢ can be spontaneous and comfortable with change.

➢ enjoys being with learners and has a heart to share God's love with them.

➢ understands the importance of helping learners become biblically literate, to know and understand the Bible and the life links that live within its stories.

➢ is committed as a leader, coach, and shepherd to disciple learners.

➢ gives of his or her time to attend leader training and equipping sessions.

➢ models the journey of a follower of Jesus.

➤ is comfortable with incorporating games in learning.

➤ comprehends the four-step process of learning through games, outlined in chapter four of this book.

➤ has been exposed to multiple intelligences information and recognizes that people learn through a wide variety of ways and means.

Of course, we hope and pray for the right leader for the right situation. We want the very best for our children. The strength of our leaders impacts the strength of the ministry.

It is important that our leaders understand their invitation to live out their call in the body of Christ. We are gifted by God and filled with unique talents.

Do all that you can to help people of all ages comprehend that they are invited to serve, that they are ignited by the Holy Spirit, and that we are all united as one body in Christ on this journey of proclaiming the good news. When discipleship and servanthood become a shared vision, then finding and mobilizing strong leaders becomes a biblical journey. When incorporating games in our curriculum, quality leadership is a vital ingredient.

Basically, don't we all want a leader who is fun to be with—who makes learners feel safe, cared for and loved? Someone who is approachable and filled with the gift of hospitality? I want a leader that looks into the eyes of each learner and sees Christ. And, I want those learners to see Christ looking back at them.

Focus #2
Safety in the Game

When playing games, we want to make sure that everyone is put in a safe situation. As I downhill ski, I want to make sure that when (not if) I fall, my boots will release from my bindings. Also, I'm guardful that my skill in skiing matches the challenge and difficulty of the run that I'm about to ski.

When I see moguls the size of Volkswagens and a ski run named Widow Maker, I know—I don't go there. I might as well stay in the chalet and squeeze my fingers with a pliers and have just as much fun—that ski run will not be safe for me and it will not be fun!

In using games in Christian education, make sure you carefully think through how the game will be played, where it will be played, who will play it, and what possible hazards or dangers might exist in the playing of it.

Consider this safety check list:

➤ Is the space a safe place for game playing?

➤ Are there pointed or sharp edges in the playing area?

➤ Is the floor slippery or bumpy? Will there be running or a lot of moving in the game? Will the learners run into each other causing collisions? How could that be avoided?

➤ Is there enough room for the game to be played?

➤ Is the equipment to be used in good, safe condition?

➤ Is the game age appropriate?

➤ Are there any objects that may be knocked over or broken?

➤ Could the ceilings, walls, or floor prove dangerous?

> *In using games in Christian education, make sure you carefully think through how the game will be played, where it will be played, who will play it, and what possible hazards or dangers might exist in the playing of it.*

➤ Is the pace of the game age appropriate?
➤ Is the leader-to-learner ratio safe?
Thinking proactively, not reactively.

The younger the learner, the more adults you need. As a general rule of thumb:
➤ Preschool: seven or eight learners per adult
➤ Kindergarten to second grade: 12 learners per adult
➤ Third to fourth grade: five learners per adult
➤ Fifth to sixth grade: 15-20 learner per adult

The above ratios apply to the physical safety of learners. We also want to be sensitive to our learner's emotional safety. Will the game experience:
➤ Be a positive one for each learner?
➤ Provide an atmosphere whereby each learner feels safe to express his or her ideas?
➤ Honor and respect each learner?
➤ Reflect God's care for the learners?
➤ Have a good mixture of active play and calm settings as a part of creating a safe place for learners?

Even Jesus told his disciples after they had been out preaching and teaching to go to a quiet place, a place of serenity and be still.

It may be helpful to mentally walk through the whole game experience to anticipate the necessary changes and adaptations to safeguard an experience for learners. Have fun with games—they are intended to be a learning resource. You may wish to tweak or change the game to meet your setting so that it is a safe experience.

I am stressing safety in this resource also because of the liability issues involved with engaging learners in activity. Along with having fun and enjoying the use of games in our curriculum, we must also be aware of any possible risk factors.

Having the right leader in place will also help to ensure a safe experience for learners. Take great care in leadership training and equipping with safety in mind.

Also, keep in mind that in addition to playing games and being active, learners need to sit and be still.

Focus #3
Tools and Gear

What supplies, tools, props, or gear will you need for the game? Will you need a Bible, climbing rope, parachute, utility balls, planks, tires, balloons, or blindfolds? Whatever supplies are necessary, make sure that they are safe, in good condition, age appropriate, and appropriate for the game.

Jesus told his disciples after they had been out preaching and teaching to go to a quiet place.

Supplies that I find helpful and like to have on hand are:

➤ beach balls
➤ a train whistle
➤ a feather
➤ a long rope
➤ paper

It seems like a simple list, but a variety of games can be played with just a few—or even no—supplies!

WE'RE READY.
LET'S SPARK THE START—LET'S LIVE IT AND LEARN IT

Enjoy the following examples of games for your Christian education. The games represent several settings for experienced learning.

#1 Hot and Cold
(For multigenerational gatherings)

Number of players:	Unlimited
Materials needed:	Two symbolic items, such as a matchbook and a Bible
Location:	This game can be played indoors or outdoors. Wherever it is played, there must be an area where one person can go out of ear shot and eyesight of the group.
Focus:	Identifying mixed messages
Learning point:	Jesus said, "I am the Way and the Truth and the Life."

This game is a variation of the popular one where the group tries to direct a learner to an item by calling out "hot" (if the learner is close to the item) or "cold" (if the learner is far away from the item). Begin by choosing one person to be "It." Ask that learner to leave the room so he or she cannot hear what the group talks about.

When the learner is out of the room, explain that the leader will hide two items within the room. You might select a matchbook (symbolic of the vices in our lives, the things that trip us up, the negative aspects of the world) and a Bible (where we want learners to be grounded). We want learners to know the Bible and live by the lessons found therein.

Now, starting with the learner next to you, number off by twos. The Number 1s will guide the person that is "It" to the Bible by shouting out "Hot!" if he or she gets close to it, and "Cold!" if he or she is far away from it. The Number 2s will do the same to guide the learner to the matchbook.

Both groups will be doing this at the same time. Of course, the learner being directed does not know that the group is divided and thus will be receiving mixed messages.

Look at the ways people want to follow their own counsel rather than rely on God in their lives.

Invite the learner back into the room. Explain the basic game of Hot and Cold. Then, let the game begin. You will see "It" getting increasingly frustrated as he or she is constantly tugged in opposite directions by the group.

Let the game process go on for a while. An item may or may not be found. After a brief time, stop the game and ask "It" how he or she is feeling during the game. Some responses may be: I feel confused and tugged in many directions; I'm not getting a clear message.

A word of caution: This can be a loud game and a difficult process. When a learner is looking for the items, be very watchful of how he or she is feeling. Don't let the game go too long. Let's not allow anyone to experience anything that is overly frustrating. I often stop this game long before an item is found and begin the debriefing.

Explain to the learner what was going on, and thank him or her with a hearty round of applause.

Talk about mixed messages—the point of this game—with the group. Do we know what mixed messages are? What mixed messages are learners, youth, and families hearing today? Learners might discuss how messages from families can conflict with messages from peers.

Look at the ways people want to follow their own counsel rather than rely on God in their lives. Look at the powerful mixed messages the media (TV, movies, books, radio, music, Internet) uses to sell items and/or influence people in today's society.

Ask the learners whether or how they contribute to the proliferation of mixed messages today. What can be done to change that direction? Jesus asks us whether we want to know the truth. He said, "I am the Way and the Truth and the Life."

This is where we, as Christian educators, bring in Scripture as the heart of why we played this game. Open your Bible and move into the its teachings that direct us in listening to God's voice.

#2 First Communion Instruction

Number of players:	Unlimited
Materials needed:	None
Location:	This game can be played indoors or outdoors.
Learning point:	Obedience to God's word

I was with a group of first to third grade learners for their first-communion instruction. The pastor was teaching the Old Testament story of Moses telling the Israelites they must pack up and be ready to move the next day. The Israelites didn't have a lot of time—they had to move fast.

The pastor leading this instruction, T.J. Anderson, invited the learners in the class to follow him as he ran outside and put his hand in the snow. (The training was in February in Minnesota!) Everyone got up when he said "Go!" and followed him at that instant. They didn't ask questions. They moved fast. They couldn't take anything, not even their coats. They were to move fast and travel light—just like the Israelites had to do when they were freed from slavery under the Pharaoh's rule.

Imagine how this activity impressed the learners. They now could relate to how the Israelites felt when they had to pack up and move out fast. For the Israelites, there was no time even to let the yeast rise in the bread—thus they had unleavened bread. This game helped the story come alive in the learners' minds.

#3 Bible Squares
(A "Hollywood Squares"-like game of tic-tac-toe)

Number of players:	Unlimited
Materials needed:	Construction scaffolding (if possible), a microphone, cards with questions for each of the nine characters, nine large cards with a big letter O one one side and a big X on the other side
People needed:	Nine costumed biblical characters, an emcee, an audience (Sunday school, Bible school, or another large church group and its leaders)
Location:	A gym or fellowship hall with space for a large-group event
Learning point:	Review of Bible characters and lessons. Are learners retaining what they are being taught?

This unique, active learning game of Bible review engages learners and adults alike as they recall Bible stories. It is based on the popular TV show "Hollywood Squares," and will require some initial set-up and volunteer recruitment to literally set the stage.

In advance: Identify nine Bible stories that students have been studying in Sunday school, and select one significant person/character from each story. Invite nine people to portray those Bible story characters. They will occupy the squares and answer learners' questions. Examples: If you have studied the story of Jonah and the whale, you could have either Jonah himself or the whale occupy a square. From the story of Ruth, the representative could be Ruth or Naomi. The story of Noah, of course, offers many choices: Noah, one of the animals, or even the dove.

Set-up: Find people who are involved with a construction company and borrow a scaffolding for the event. *Make sure it is safe!* You might choose to decorate the scaffolding with draped lengths of fabric or whatever you have on hand to make it festive and fun. Set up the scaffolding in nine squares created like a tic-tac-toe game.

The emcee will begin the event by dividing the group into two teams (the Xs and the Os). Characters should be in position in the squares at this time. Then the first team selects someone to go to the front of the room and choose one of the characters in the squares.

The emcee will then read a statement or ask a question of that character about his or her role in the Bible. The character may tell the truth or give a false answer.

Bible Squares

The learner that asked the question turns to the team and they decide together whether the character's response is true or false. If the team decides correctly, the character in that square holds up the team's card (an X or O). If the team decides incorrectly, no card is displayed; play moves to the next team.

Now the opposite team takes a turn, following the same procedure. Teams alternated turns, each time announcing a square and a possible intention (for example: "I'll take Noah" or "I'll take Moses to block"). The game continues as a game of tic-tac-toe would. Remember, in the game of tic-tac-toe, sometimes there is a winner, and sometimes there is not.

During the game, you might stop for "commercials" to announce upcoming church or Sunday school events, encourage readership of children's ministry newsletters or other church publications, or advertise special church items (for example: T-shirts, water bottles, visors). Keep the commercials fun and lively with announcements such as, "Our program is brought to you today by Offering Envelopes."

#4 Target Toss

Number of players:	Unlimited (If the group is too large, split it in two.)
Materials needed:	Wadded-up pieces of paper, one wastebasket
Location:	Indoors or outdoors
Learning point:	Get to know God's Word. Be on target with where God wants you to be.

Put a wastebasket on one side of the room. Have the class gather on the other side of the room, far away from the target. Give each learner several pieces of wadded-up paper.

When you signal "go," everyone begins trying to toss the paper balls into the wastebasket. A long distance will make this very difficult. Gradually, learners move closer to the target, taking one giant step at a time when the leader indicates. Eventually, the learners will be standing very close to the basket—maybe even right over the basket—so that the paper wads go into it easily.

The object here is that we want to get closer and closer to knowing God's Word and God's way so that we can be right on target in living our lives as followers of Jesus. After the game, sit down and discuss a Bible story. We want to be in the Bible, studying it, and learning from it!

#5 Circle Dodge Ball

Number of players:	Unlimited (If the group is too large, split it in two.)
Materials needed:	10-15 small rubber balls or tennis balls
Location:	Indoors or outdoors
Learning point:	Teamwork, God's love and care for us

Have the learners sit on the floor in a big circle. One learner is asked to volunteer to stand in the center of the circle. Give out 10 to 15 balls to the learners in the circle. Direct the learners to roll all the balls at once, trying to hit the shoes of the one in the middle. The one in the middle may move all over, trying to avoid being hit. Learners may roll the balls only—no throwing! The balls must remain on the floor.

What will happen? Almost all of the balls touch the person because she or he can't get out of the way of so many balls. Keep the balls going constantly—

learners in the circle continue to roll the balls back and forth across the circle.

After a while, stop all the balls. Ask several learners to enter the circle and form a protective ring around the learner in the center. Have the learners remaining in the outside circle begin rolling the balls again.

What happens this time? The protective ring of learners keep the balls away from hitting the learner. That learner can stand there, confident in not getting hit.

Now have all the learners sit down. Read the story of Daniel in the Lion's den. Next, discuss how the learner in the middle was kept safe by the ones who were protecting him or her. Relate that to how God protected Daniel in the lion's den. How does God protect us? How might we help to protect others at home, at school, wherever we are? Daniel was faithful to God. He prayed to God.

We also want to be faithful to God. We pray for God to protect us and our family, friends, and those around the world. We live in a world where there is sin. Someday, we will be with God in heaven where there is no sin.

#6 Beach Ball Toss

Number of players:	Unlimited (If the group is too large, break down into smaller groups)
Materials needed:	Large beach balls
Location:	Indoors or outdoors
Learning point:	Teamwork, working together as disciples

Gather everyone in a group and have them sit scattered on the floor. The leader tosses in a large beach ball and everyone works together to keep the ball up in the air as long as possible. You might choose to add a challenge by having the learners count the number of times they hit the ball.

Set a goal of keeping the ball in the air up to the count of 10, 25, or 50. If the ball drops, start over again, counting at 0. Remember not to let anyone feel bad if they miss or cause the ball to drop.

Stress creative teamwork. This game can be used as a lead-in to teach a Sunday school session, or it can be played before or after a major event. Players can be added or subtracted easily as they arrive to class or are picked up at the end of class.

Process:
> ➢ What helped to keep the ball up in the air?
> ➢ Did everyone have an opportunity to hit the ball?
> ➢ What would happen if we added another ball or many balls?
> ➢ Was the game fun?
> ➢ Was it difficult?
> ➢ What does it mean to be part of a team?
> ➢ How do you think the disciples worked together as a team?

➤ What does it mean to be a follower of Jesus today? What happens when we work together? What happens when we don't work together?

CLOSING

Learning through games will be an ongoing process and a continuous journey of learning throughout our lives. Learners will experience games and then we, as their leader, shepherd, and coach, will draw out their reactions to those experiences. We will help them to look both within and outward.

Know that as a learner journeys from the time with you, he or she does not leave the same person as when the time began. By being with you and being taught by you, the learner's life is changed. Praise God for the journey!

Well, how is the fire burning? Keep your passion lit for sharing God's love with learners.

May God richly bless your time spent in teaching through games to, for, and with learners.

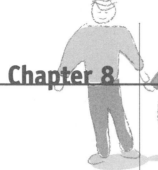

Chapter 8

How Games Are Woven into a Sunday School Session

Let's dig in a bit deeper. The following session examples illustrate how games may be woven into a Sunday school curriculum. Please note that each of these examples was originally preceded by a large-group celebration, gathering all the learners and their leaders. There was music, prayer, candle lighting, skits, seed planting of the theme of the day, a collection of offerings, fellowship, a time to invite everyone into a common focus, and praising of Jesus' name.

The learning process now becomes a multifaceted journey:

- listening
- stillness
- moving
- laughing
- singing
- changing spaces
- movement from a large-group setting to a small-group setting, gathering by grade or in smaller groups by grade
- total mind and body involvement
- speaking
- sharing
- learning
- lifting out individual ideas and thoughts
- facing different directions
- giving and receiving
- standing up and sitting down
- playing
- praying
- praising God
- having fun
- hearing about God
- formulating values
- receiving God's Word
- building relationships
- connecting with God's people
- worship
- study
- being very active
- surprise

Look for these elements as you move through the examples provided here. Watch how the games add to the session and affect the learning process. What would the sessions be like without the games and activities? (I rest my case!)

Examples of entire session plans are provided to show how you might travel from beginning to end with a teaching theme and an educational focus. Take note of:

- where games are placed in the session for pace and interest.
- the process questions used to bring out a Bible message.
- the simplicity of the games.
- what supplies were required and what space was necessary.

The curriculum ideas presented here are designed for first to sixth grade. Notes will be made throughout these sessions to help focus your attention on the flow of the curriculum. These notes will be in italics.

Session Example 1

Chapter 9

BAPTISM OF JESUS

Luke 3:1-38 (Particularly verses 21 and 22);
Mark 1:1-11 (Basis of the session)

Good Mooooorning, Leaders!

(Motivation, encouragement, gratitude, and affirmation)

You, the leader, are the backbone of our Sunday school! We are so very grateful that you are here. Thank you. Today we're looking at the baptism of Jesus—the beginning of his ministry, travels, and teachings.

Important Ingredients

(Focus help)

➤ Scripture reference:
Luke 3:1-38 (especially verses 21 and 22) and Mark 1:1-11

First to Third Grade

(Focus help)

To begin, you will gather in a large group. The following elements will be incorporated into a children's worship or celebration time. The staff will lead this time.

➤ Welcome
➤ Candles
➤ Prayer
➤ Songs
➤ Introduction to story
➤ Offering

Then, you will move into a smaller group setting according to grade. Gather your crew! Discuss with fellow leaders:

➤ Any personal memories of being baptized.
➤ Baptisms you have seen. Who/when/where was it?
➤ Other baptism stories (that of their own children, godchildren, nieces, nephews, or friends)

Leaders may want to continually assess the leaders' journey of implementing games by asking the following questions:

* *How is Sunday school going so far?*
* *What are your concerns or frustrations?*
* *What are your successes?*

The Bible in Action

(An active game that provides a good
energy ingredient at this point in the session)

Next, the following props will be available for you. (Please be sure to leave them for the next class when you are finished with this activity.)

➤ Blue streamers
➤ White streamers
➤ Plain paper—rolled and taped to create a megaphone

Begin reading from Mark 1. Read verses 1-8. Talk to the learners about John the Baptist as you go through these verses. John preached in the wilderness of Judea near the Jordan River, and was:

➤ the son of Elizabeth and Zechariah.
➤ a cousin of Jesus.
➤ six months older than Jesus.
➤ a well-known prophet.

When you come to verses 9-11, bring in the props. Hand out some of the props to the learners. They will listen for your directions (below in italics).

	LEADER SAYS:	LEARNERS DO:
Verse 9:	At that time Jesus came from Nazareth in Galilee and was baptized by John in the Jordan.	*Make low waves with the blue streamers like we are in a river.*
Verse 10:	As John was coming up out of the water, he saw the heaven being torn open and the Spirit descending on him like a dove.	*Wave the blue streamers above your head. This is the sky. On the word* opened, *slowly lower the blue streamers. Wave the white streamer above your head. This is the dove. Make the dove fly above and then lower it to your shoulder.*
Verse 11:	And a voice came from heaven: "And this is my son, with whom I am well pleased."	*Now pick up your megaphone. Use the megaphone to say, "This is my son with whom I am well pleased." Repeat this line two times.*

God wants us to believe in his son Jesus. God is very pleased with his son.

Echo Prayer

(Continues to keep everyone involved with their whole body)

LEADER:	LEARNERS:
Dear God,	*Dear God,*
Thank you for	*Thank you for*
sending me	*sending me*

Your son
Jesus Christ.
I know
that Jesus loves me
and I want
to love and follow Jesus.
Please lead me, God,
and thank you for
loving me!

Your son
Jesus Christ.
I know
that Jesus loves me
and I want
to love and follow Jesus.
Please lead me, God,
and thank you for
loving me!

John 3:16

(A movement activity that enhances memory and retention what's been taught)

LEADER SAYS:	LEARNERS DO:
For God so loved the world	*Stretch your arms way out. Now bring them in with a huge hug. God loves us so much!*
that he gave his only son	*Now bring your arms out as in a giving motion—as God gave us his son.*
that whoever believes in him	*Now put one hand on your head and one hand on your heart—as we love Jesus will all our heart and with all our mind.*
will never die	*Roll your arms around and over each other—our spirit will live forever.*
but have eternal life.	*Everyone clap at a 10!* In fact, let's all say, "Praise God!"*
	* Explained on page 21 ("O'Meter Warm-Up").

Let's learn a verse—John 3:16. To help remember this verse, let's try the following actions:

Baptism Discussion

(More information is given here than will actually be necessary, but a prepared leader will use this information throughout the whole session.)

At this point, please discuss baptism with your class. Use some of the following information:

What is the sacrament of Baptism?

➢ It's an act of God that unites us with the risen Christ and makes us members of God's family.

➢ Through water filled with the power of God's Word, Baptism:
1. Washes away the guilt of our sins.
2. Bestows God's grace upon us.
3. Delivers us from the power of death.
4. Promises us eternal life in God's kingdom.

➢ Through baptism, we are reborn as children of God. We become sisters and brothers in a new family that includes Christians all over the world.

Therefore, if anyone is in Christ, he is a new creation; the old has gone, the new has come. (2 Corinthians 5:17)

We can follow the journey of Baptism in the Bible.

➢ In the Old Testament, people washed themselves during ceremonies with water to purify their bodies in obedience to God's law.

➢ John the Baptist baptized people in the River Jordan. He called people to repent. He told people: "I baptize you with water. But one more powerful than I will come, the thongs of whose sandals I am not worthy to untie. He will baptize you with the Holy Spirit and with fire." (Luke 3:16)

➢ Jesus' baptism was by John in the River Jordan. Read Luke 3:21-22. A voice spoke from heaven and the Holy Spirit filled Jesus.

➢ After Jesus' resurrection, the disciples were told to go and make disciples and baptize all nations. Read Matthew 28:19.

Baptism

➢ Baptism joins water and God's Word to give us life, forgiveness, and salvation.

➢ People may be baptized at any age, but need to receive the sacrament only once in their lifetime.

➢ Parents are to nourish their children's spiritual growth—teach them to pray, provide for their child's baptism, and build their family with kindness, respect, and forgiveness in the Spirit.

➢ The church community—or, according to Martin Luther, "the mother of all believers"—is to celebrate Baptism in keeping the promise to welcome the newly baptized and to give them support so that the membership grows in faith and understanding. We are to share the Word of God, live a Christian life, and give of our time and talents.

➢ The role of sponsors is to set an example of Christian life and service. They are to pray for that child and encourage him or her to lead a Christian life. They often present the child at the Holy Baptism celebration.

Picture Review

(Game to provide learners with a break from listening and sitting)

To end this teaching time, you will have five pictures. Select five learners to come forward to hold the following pictures (these can be simple line drawings, or collected from old Sunday school curriculum, or a mix) in front of their chests.

- Jesus greeting John, who is standing in the water
- John baptizing Jesus in the water
- The heavens opening up
- The dove descending upon Jesus
- A reference to God's words about his Son

Scramble the pictures as you hand them out. *Do not* have them in sequential order. Ask one or two students to put the pictures in order, according to the story of Jesus being baptized.

Note: Help where necessary, but try not to help too much. Tell the class to remain silent. When finished, congratulate and thank everyone for helping.

Shower and Bath—Washing

(Activity that takes session home)

Tell the learners that whenever they shower or take a bath, or wash their face and hands, to think about their baptism and how they are blessed by God. We are baptized by the Spirit! Now, return to your tables.

Baptism Necklaces

(Whole-body art project with a message)

We will be making necklaces with leather and beads today. Supplies will be there for you.

Symbolic reasons for the necklace:

Circle: The necklace is a circle of leather around your neck and the bead is a circular shape. A circle never ends, just like God's love for you.

Unique: Even though all the necklaces are circles and are made the same, each necklace will *still* be different and unique, just like each child of God.

The word BEAD stands for:

B less
E veryone
A nd
D iscover God's love

Steps to make the necklace:

1. Choose a piece of leather.
2. Choose a bead (one bead per learner).
3. String the bead on the leather.
4. Tie a good square knot with the leather so the bead won't fall off.
5. As the necklace is put on each learner, use the learner's name and say: (*Learner's name*) is a child of God, whom God loves dearly."

Shell Symbol

(Something to hold and feel)

Next, explain that a shell is used as a symbol for Baptism. You will see it in banners and on paraments used in churches.

Give each learner one shell. They are to hold this shell in the palm of their hand as you close with the following echo prayer.

Echo Prayer

(Brings learners voices into prayer)

LEADER:	LEARNERS:
Dear God,	*Dear God,*
We praise you.	*We praise you.*
We love you.	*We love you.*
Thank you for	*Thank you for*
sending us	*sending us*
your son Jesus.	*your son Jesus.*
We know	*We know*
that Jesus is	*that Jesus is*
The way,	*the way,*
The truth,	*the truth,*
and the life.	*and the life.*
Thank you for loving us.	*Thank you for loving us.*
We love you.	*We love you.*
Amen.	*Amen.*

THE TEMPTATION OF JESUS

Luke 4:1-13 (Basis of the session)

Good Mooooorning, Leaders!

(Connection and relationship building; ministering to those who will minister)

Today we're looking into Luke 4:1-13, the temptation of Jesus. I read this passage and began to reflect on the "right now" of my life. I look at all the things that tempt me. There are many things that tug at me. I wish I could report to you that I am as strong could ever be, but that would not be the truthful case.

I do find, however (as I'm sure you do too), that as we grow in our faith, we also grow in knowing more and more of what God has created us for and what our call is—and thus know more of the joy that we can truly experience when we are obedient to God's direction. For me, that means living within God's boundaries and stepping into the freedom and light of servanthood.

I remember years back when we invited Kathryn Koob to speak. Kathryn (as some of you may recall) was one of the two women taken hostage in Iran in 1979. She wrote a very moving book titled *Faith Under Fire*. I remember her telling us about being held in a room with only a cot, a table, and a chair. Outside her door, she was guarded 24 hours a day by soldiers armed with guns.

Kathryn said that her captors took everything away from her. But, what they could *not* take away from her were all the scripture verses, hymns, and Bible stories that she had learned throughout her whole life. They were her lifeline as she endured the wait for freedom.

Kathryn's words had an impact on my life, creating a desire to fill my life with scripture, hymns, and Bible stories to make this a life-long journey, so that through my life's journey, I may draw on God's Word and direction.

As we look at our story today, we will focus on the temptations that Jesus faced. But, also in this story, we will focus on what we can do when we're faced with those things in life that are not life-giving or Christ-centered. Let's guide our learners in learning scripture on which to build their life and decisions.

Also, as we read our story today, may we all be reminded again that we *will* sin, we *will* trip up, but God's abundant forgiveness, mercy, and grace are lovingly offered to us as we bring our sins to Christ Jesus.

May your experience today be a blessing to you and your learners. Thank you again for leading. Sue

---

Leaders should remember to ask themselves the following questions:

- *Were directions clear and understandable?*
- *Is everyone participating?*
- *Was there enough discussion time?*
- *Did the learners understand the lesson?*

First to Sixth Grade
Welcome and Prayer

(Guides a group in the ministry of hospitality)

Welcome your learners and your team. Invite learners to share their faith. Start with a prayer. Ask if there are a few learners who would like to lead the prayer. Ask them to come forward and begin, finishing the prayer with, "In your name, Lord." I hope that our learners are growing in prayer and feel open and comfortable in praying out loud. You serve as wonderful models for them.

Under-Your-Feet Balloon Burst Game

(A strong learning style to lead them into the session theme. Be sure to check for latex allergies before beginning this activity.)

Ask your learners: "What are some things in life that are tempting and not good for us?" Write things the learners list on a balloon. (Marker and balloon will be provided.) Some responses may be:

➤ Cheating
➤ Teasing
➤ Drinking under age
➤ Not allowing someone else to succeed
➤ Taking credit for someone else's work
➤ Not sharing
➤ Disobeying
➤ Being mean to someone
➤ Lying to someone
➤ Using illegal drugs
➤ Hitting
➤ Excluding or shunning someone
➤ Stealing
➤ Smoking under age
➤ Not forgiving someone
➤ Putting blame on innocent person
➤ Being deceitful
➤ Gossiping
➤ Ignoring someone
➤ Hurting someone

Talk through some of these responses. Help your learners see how we are making choices every day! Do we give into temptation and Satan *or* do we live as Jesus wants us to do?

Now, read Romans 16:19. Read it a couple times. Ask students who have Bibles to look it up. Talk about this verse:

"I want you to understand what is good and have nothing to do with evil. Then God, who gives peace, will soon crush Satan—where?—under your feet."

Now, place that balloon on the floor and say to the learners: "God does not want us to do these things. God is with us to help us make decisions. It's not easy, but God is strong. We *will* sin, we *will* make mistakes. But through the power of the Holy Spirit, we can stomp on—say no to—those things that tempt us to do wrong."

Then, the leader (or learners) will pop that balloon by stomping on it. Let this signify stomping on those things that are not good for us. Temptations be gone! (Supply a balloon to each learner.)

Note: Sometimes the balloon might slip out from underfoot. Get a nice, hearty foothold on that balloon.

Scripture with Props Game

(Game to continue and build on the experience of learning)

Read Luke 4:1-13. As you read, talk about the story.

Verses 1-3:

Jesus was hungry. He had gone 40 days with no food. But he was filled with the Holy Spirit.

Have a learner come forward and imagine that he or she is very hungry! Say: "You have gone a weekend with no food. Can you imagine one *week* with no food? Twenty days? More than a month!? Would you still be alive?"

This learner represents great hunger. Ask the learner to stay up front. Give him or her a huge donut; the learner should *not* eat that donut. Continue reading.

Verses 4-7:

As you read this passage, have another learner come up. Hand that learner some money. Jesus was offered a lot—status, wealth, authority, and money. Ask the learner to just hold the money up. Continue reading.

Verses 9-13:

Another learner will come forward. Hand him or her an inflated balloon and a stick pin (or safety pin, with younger learners). Tell the learner not to pop the balloon—even though it would be easy to do.

Review of Significant Verses

(Reinforces the session being taught)

Now, after all of the verses are read, review them. Reflect on the learners holding the props:

Verse 4: Acknowledge the learner with the donut.

The donut looks very tempting. Jesus said to Satan: Man does not live by bread alone. Jesus could have had all the food he wanted, but he would not be tempted by Satan. He would not fall under Satan's pressure.

Take the donut away from the learner.

Verse 8: Acknowledge the learner with the money.

What do we worship? Could it be that money or wealth? Sometimes numbers hold great value for us. Do we think that people are better or more important if they have a lot of money? Do we think we could find happiness if only we had more money? Can money buy love, respect, or joy?

Some people believe that money can buy *anything.* God's children do not believe that—we are to worship only God!

Take the money away from the learner.

Verse 12: Acknowledge the person with the balloon.

It would be so easy to pop that balloon, just as it would have been easy for Jesus to throw himself down from the highest point. Satan was saying, I dare you! But Jesus did not give into Satan. Jesus was filled with the Holy Spirit.

Have the learner put down the pin and take away the balloon.

Put the props away and thank the learners that helped. Note: Please get *serious* with this session.

Salt Dough Sunday

(Keeps learners involved with multiple senses)

Our sessions today and last week (the baptism of Jesus) are stories of the beginning of Jesus' ministry. How exciting these stories are. They are filled with emotion of:

➢ the heavens opening up.
➢ a dove descending from heaven.
➢ God's voice: *This is my son!*
➢ John and Jesus at the river.
➢ baptism and commitment.
➢ living in the desert.
➢ a 40-day fast.
➢ huge temptation when feeling weak, tired, and hungry.
➢ Satan wanting Jesus to fail.
➢ being faithful to God.
➢ Knowing who you are in God.

What a Journey!

Jesus was tempted with the idea of turning a stone into bread. Let's look at a story about a form of bread—the pretzel—and how someone used a pretzel for a good purpose. The pretzel was turned into a message of care and love in the following story.

The Legend of the Pretzel

Somewhere in a northern Italy or southern France monastery, a monk took some leftover strips of bread dough and twisted them to resemble arms folded over the breast in prayer. The monk baked the twisted dough strips and awarded them to children who learned their prayers well. He called his baked bread "pretiola" but today it is known as "pretzel."

The pretiola quickly became popular in bakeries throughout Europe, especially in Germany, Austria, and later in America, where the name "pretzel" became trendy.

When the Turks were trying to seize Vienna in 1510, the city's pretzel bakers, preparing the next day's batch, heard the enemy tunneling late at night under the city walls. The bakers quickly gathered weapons, charged the Turks in the tunnels, and annihilated them. In thanks, the Viennese king bestowed a coat of arms on the pretzel baker. The emblem, which depicts a lion holding a shield with the form of a pretzel in its center, still hangs outside every Austrian pretzel bakery.

Pretzel Project

Materials for this project will be supplied.

Invite the learner to make a pretzel, *not for eating*, but as a reminder of God's loving arms guiding us through each and every day of our lives. A pretzel could also remind them of arms folded in prayer.

Sculpt the dough on a paper plate.

Pretzel Project

Third to Sixth Grade Challenge
(Ignites learners to think about and translate their faith through experiential learning)

This is a challenge for our older learners. Instead of simply creating a pretzel shape, they are to search creatively for a shape of something that will be an icon of sorts for them in thinking about our session today.

Here are some examples of things they could make:

➢ Cross—Put a hole in the top of it so that they could string leather or ribbon through it. They could hang the cross in their room, in a hallway, or in a place where they would see it as a reminder of where it is Christ wants them to walk and who it is Christ wants them to be.

➢ Heart—to remind them of Christ's love.

➢ Tree—with the significance of growing in Christ.

➢ Candle—being the light of Christ's love in the world.

➢ Letters—of a word to inspire them. The sky is the limit as to what they could spell.

Note: Please be mindful of the amount of salt dough that we have for the whole morning. Please give a small fist-sized amount (approx. ¾ cup to one cup) of salt dough to each learner. Ration all of these supplies sensibly. Thank you for your cooperation in this area.

Have the learners take their project home and bake it at 350° F (180° C) for one hour. You might send home a sheet clearly explaining the baking instructions and reminding learners not to place their creation on the paper plate in the microwave. Remind students not to bake the dough on a paper plate!

Have fun! Be creative! Please be very careful that the salt dough gets off the floor in your room. Again, have fun!

Lean-On-Me Closing

(A very active game that involves the whole body and mind in learning; guaranteed to bring about lots of laughter and fun)

We must look to each other for help and care. Let's help each other walk the walk that Jesus wants us to. Let's lean on each other for support!

Have learners sit down on the floor in pairs, back to back, elbows linked, knees bent, and feet flat on the floor. (If you have an odd number, take turns trying this.) Next, tell the learners to lean on each other and use their feet to lightly push into each other and then slowly stand. Be careful—show Christian support.

Lean-On-Me Closing

Note: You may want to have two people demonstrate this first. Matching learners of similar height and weight helps. Make this comfortable and not embarrassing. Be alert to things like short skirts, very shy learners, and so forth.

Talk to the learners about the need to support each other:

➤ We all need support.

➤ We all need to feel wanted.

➤ Do the learners know people who don't feel as though they are loved, really wanted, or included?

➤ It is our call from God to lend our support, love, and care to those around us, as well as those around the world. Remember the pretzel arms—love, pray, and care for others.

Jesus was filled with the Holy Spirit. May *we* be filled with the Holy Spirit. And when we're tempted to ignore, gossip, shun, steal, hurt, or hit—may we have the power of the Holy Spirit to STOMP that temptation right under our feet!

Jesus Christ is Lord and King! Amen

End in prayer. This is an opportunity to reinforce the session theme. Invite learners to pray too.

Session Example 3

Chapter 11

THE PARABLES

Basis of study: The Lost Sheep (Luke 15:1-7);
The Lost Coin (Luke 15:8-10); The Lost Son (Luke 15:11-32)

Amazing grace, how sweet the sound,
That saved a wretch like me.
I once was lost, but now I'm found.
Was blind, but now I see.

Greetings, Everyone!

(Affirm and thank)

Thank you for all that you do. Thank you for giving of who you are—who God has created you to be. Please let us know how we may serve you. We pray that you will have a morning filled with blessings of energy and joy in the Lord!

Let's all be on the same page in our ministry walk—that we seek to create an experience for everyone of:

➢ Physical and emotional safety. We are a place of God's grace.

➢ Fun and celebration. Let's get our hearts smiling and laughing—true joy in the Lord!

➢ True care and respect for everyone. Use good manners, be polite, show God's care.

Warm-Up

(Game that invites learners to be actively involved)

Gather your learners in a listening group and welcome them to Sunday school. Toss these questions out to the entire group:

➢ What was the most fun thing they did all week?

➢ Did anyone help another person this week?

You may listen to a few learner responses, or you may invite learners to turn to the person next to them and pair-share their answers. Or you may do both.

Leaders should remember to ask themselves the following questions:

- *Were directions clear and understandable?*
- *Is everyone participating?*
- *Was there enough discussion time?*
- *Did the learners understand the lesson?*

Prayer

(A most vital ingredient throughout the whole learning experience)

Open with a prayer. You may use an echo prayer, or a leader-led prayer, or a combination of ways.

Hot & Cold

(A very active game, placed at a strategic spot as a way to help teach the day's Bible stories)

Ask for one brave learner to leave the room and go into a "soundproof booth" (a space away from your class area where your conversation can't be heard). Make sure an adult or another helper goes out with the learner. You just want that learner to be out of the room so that you may explain the game.

When that student has left, explain the game of Hot & Cold. Choose one item that you want the learner to identify—a chair, marker, Bible, lamp, or something else. Everyone in the room will know what the item has been chosen.

Next, tell the class that when the learner comes back in the room he or she will try to guess the item by having the class guide him or her to the object. The class will *only* guide the learner by saying "Hot" or "Cold," according to the learner's proximity to the object ("hot" for near, "cold" for distant). Students may also use terms like "burning" and "freezing."

When the learner comes back in, explain the game. Begin the game—the learner should move all over the room and listen for "hot" and "cold" cues from the class. The learner may pick up things and ask, "Is this it?" When the learner identifies the object (don't make it too hard for them to guess), the whole class should celebrate—clap hands and cheer for the learner.

Scripture Focus:
To God, People Are a Prize!

(Process time)

Explain that today's Bible stories are about things being lost and then found. Ask the class: Have you ever lost something—but then found it again?

Read Luke 15:1-7, the story of the lost sheep. Involve learners with the story.

After reading the story, hold up a stack of 100 paper plates (provided for you). Remove one plate. How many are left? (*99.*) There are plenty of plates left.

So why worry about one plate being gone? Well, maybe there is a grand party planned and there are 100 special people invited. Each guest must have a plate so we would look for that one lost plate and when we found the plate, we would be glad!

Jesus told stories called Parables. Tell the learner that a parable is an earthly story with a heavenly meaning! Jesus told stories to help us learn. The story of the lost sheep is a parable.

When the shepherd found the sheep, there was a celebration. Just like when people learn about Jesus and then believe in Jesus, they have found Jesus. Jesus loves each person and wants each person to love him.

We share in the joy that Jesus offers us. To Jesus, we are his treasures, his precious children. We are very, very important to him—he loves us dearly. Jesus celebrates as we love and serve him.

Read the short parable of the lost coin from Luke 15:8-10. The coin was lost, then it was found, and the woman celebrated!

Then read another parable. This one is about the prodigal son. Read Luke 15:11-31 with a lot of animation and passion. This is another great story of lost and found, and it is another story of celebration. The son was found—he came home!

When we are tempted to do wrong, we are not living how Jesus wants us to live. When we say that we are sorry to Jesus, he welcomes us into his arms with great joy. He forgives us, just like the dad welcomed his son.

Paper Plate Faces Game

Every learner will make two paper plates with faces—one happy face and one sad face. Show the plate with the sad face. This person has sinned. He or she was teasing someone at school and made the other person cry because the teasing really hurt that person's feelings.

Next show the plate with the happy face. This is the person who teased another person but he or she prayed to Jesus, saying: "Jesus, I'm so very sorry that I teased someone today at school. I am so sorry that I made that person cry. I feel so sad, Jesus. I'm sorry. Please forgive me. Help me to be kind and caring to others. I'm going to tell that person that I'm sorry and I'm going to be respectful and caring towards that person."

Jesus said: "I forgive you, my child. I love you."

And there's the smile on that child's face. If you do wrong, don't stay miserable. Pray to God to forgive your sins! God celebrates when we find our way in prayer.

Ask the learners, "Is there something that *you* want to tell God that you're sorry about? Let's all pray."

Fold hands and close eyes. The leader may lead the prayer: Dear God, forgive us for the things we do that are wrong, for the things we do that hurt others. We are sorry, God. Please forgive us. Amen!

Remember the shepherd who lost one sheep. The shepherd was happy when he had all the sheep back in his flock. Jesus wants all of us to be in his flock—not sinning or lost, but right with him doing what Jesus would do.

Invite the learner to create stories using the paper plates to demonstrate people disobeying. Then have them create a story of people obeying God.

Jesus Celebrates and Loves ME!

(Activity that draws on the learners' creativity and imagination)

Markers, crayons, pencils, and a handout will be provided for this activity.

I remember seeing a poster from the LifeKeys training. This is a training on Myers-Briggs, spiritual gifts, and our passions. It was a poster that my friend made—a poster all about her. I thought it was awesome. Our celebration project with the learners today is to make a wonderful poster of the wonderful learners they are.

Give each learner a large piece of paper to design a creative poster that portrays who they are. They are to make this poster with drawings and words. Have learners consider some of the following topics to include on their posters:

➢ What they just love to do
➢ Things they do well
➢ Their favorite food
➢ Their favorite color
➢ Their family
➢ Their friends
➢ Where they love to go
➢ What they like to play
➢ What makes them happy
➢ What makes them sad

Encourage the learners to be creative and soar with their ideas. Remind them that each person is unique, wonderful, special, and amazing to God. God celebrates each one of us!

Closing

(Brings everyone together for a time of focus on the session's goals and objectives)

Call for everyone's attention. Tell the class: "We had three stories today—about the sheep, coin, and son. How were the stories the same? How were they different? What happened at the end of each story?

When we sin or do wrong or stray from God's way, what should we do? (*Pray and ask for forgiveness.*) What will Jesus do? (*Forgive us and welcome us into his arms.*)

Stretch 'n' Praise

(An important way to move learners in a meaningful manner)

The leader will lead this game by giving these directions:

➢ Everybody stand up.
➢ Stretch to the ceiling.
➢ Clap your hands.
➢ Jump up and down lightly as you clap.
➢ Everyone say "Yeah!" as you jump and clap.
➢ Get louder!
➢ Now, freeze and stop!

It's great to celebrate and be happy. When we are a part of God's family and are doing what Jesus would do, we feel happy inside and outside!

Lord's Prayer

(An interjection of one of the foundation prayers that we want learners to know)

Sit together and pray the Lord's Prayer. After the prayer, learners may continue to work on their posters if they need to wait to be picked up.

RESULTS

Our leaders and learners alike found these sessions to be engaging and very helpful in learning biblical truths. They all agreed that games are deeply beneficial as a learning tool for Christian education because they:

➤ involve the whole person of the learner.
➤ create energy in the session.
➤ allow learners to use their minds.
➤ make Sunday school a fun experience.

Chapter 12

Games and Multiple Intelligences

Let's go on a journey of looking at what the Multiple Intelligences are about. In 1983, Howard Gardner of Harvard University wrote a book titled *Frames of Mind: The Theory of Multiple Intelligences*. In his book, Gardner points out that each human being learns differently, using different "intelligences." This study encourages us to look at two driving ideas.

One is that we are not fixed for life with the intelligences that we are born with. We have the ability to grow in our intellectual capacity. Secondly, there is not only one way to be smart. Thus, Gardner identified eight specific intelligences. They are: verbal/linguistic, musical, visual/spatial, interpersonal, intrapersonal, bodily/kinesthetic, logical/mathematical, and naturalist.

As we teach learners in our Christian education arena, it is important to focus on the unique and diverse learning styles of each learner. Each learner has his or her individual gifts, talents, and abilities to be celebrated.

In each group of learners gathered for Sunday school, we know that there will be a representation of all the multiple intelligences. We also know that leaders who are teaching learners in Christian education will represent the multiple intelligences. And so, to be on the cutting edge of teaching the good news, we need to be cognizant of involving experiences that lift up the multiple intelligences. We want to make understanding of the Bible accessible to all students. We want each learner to become all that God has created him or her to be. We bless each learner when we place great value on the uniqueness of individual learning styles.

The following are suggestions as to how games may be woven into a Christian education curriculum to lift up the multiple intelligences.

VERBAL/LINGUISTIC

Game Idea: Progressive Bible Story

The leader will teach a story from the Bible (use a Bible storybook with younger learners). Spend time learning as much of the story as possible. When you think that the learners know the story well, bring them into the following creative game.

One learner will begin telling the story (the leader begins for younger learners). After a few sentences, that person will stop and then the next person will pick up wherever the first person left off. The more learners play this game, the

The games listed in this chapter can be adapted for all grade levels. For example, the Line Tag game can be played with the youngest learner to the oldest with slight modifications. Options at the end of each game are also easily adaptable.

better they will become at it. Make it fun by having the one speaking stop in the middle of a sentence. Be careful that a learner is not placed in an embarrassing position if they don't remember the story. Encourage everyone!

Other Verbal/Linguistic Activities:

➢ Use a game-show format like "Jeopardy" or "Who Wants to Be a Disciple?" to teach the Bible.

➢ Share jokes and puns that use Bible stories or characters.

➢ Create a cheer for your church or use the theme "Come to Church!"

MUSICAL

Game Idea: Name That Tune!

Materials: musical instruments or microphone

Music is a wonderful way to learn Scripture. We praise God through music. We pray through music. The leader of this game will play a few notes or sing a few notes from a Christian song. The class will then try to guess the name of the song. You may play this as teams.

Other Musical Activities:

➢ Play music as you pray or read Scripture.

➢ Turn a Bible story into a fun opera! Every word must be sung!

➢ Put a Bible story a familiar tune such as "Jingle Bells," "Twinkle, Twinkle Little Star," or "Happy Birthday to You." This may be done as a team.

VISUAL/SPATIAL

Game Idea: Bible Story Mix-Up!

Materials: markers, crayons, 11" x 14" (28 x 35 cm) sheets of paper

Using a Bible story the class has studied, have learners draw the story. Each learner should draw one scene from the story. Collect the completed drawings and hand them out randomly, picture side down, to learners in the class.

Ask each learner to turn over his or her picture. Without using words, the learners are to assemble themselves into a line or a circle so the drawings are in correct sequential order.

After the game is completed, engage the class in a discussion of how they communicated with each other to complete this task.

Other Visual/Spatial Activities:

➢ Design your own children's ministries or Sunday school T-shirts.

➢ Create a floor map of Abraham's travels. Then walk the map as you "live" the story. Use a variety of characters to create more maps.

➢ Go on a photography journey by taking pictures of all God's children or God's creation.

INTERPERSONAL

Game idea: Turn the Towel

Materials: One large beach towel for each group of seven or eight learners

This is a fun team-building game. Invite about seven or eight students to stand on a beach towel. Their mission is to turn the beach towel over to the opposite side without having anyone step off it. If someone steps off the towel, the whole group must start over again.

The emphasis of the game is to try to cooperate as a team, to communicate in a positive way, and to build relationships. Jesus built a team of disciples. We are part of a discipleship team!

Other Interpersonal Activities:

➢ Interview a Christian mentor. Share your discoveries as a class.

➢ Plan a worship service as a team.

➢ Invite another congregation to visit your Sunday school. Then go visit another church.

INTRAPERSONAL

Game Idea: Prayer Pillow

Materials: fabric pocket squares, small pillows

Give each learner a pillow. Supply a pocket-shaped piece of fabric that may be sewn or glued onto the pillow. The pillow will go home with each learner. At home, the family members will write prayers and blessings for the learner on a piece of paper, then place the folded pieces of paper in the pocket of the Prayer Pillow. The learner, with a parent or guardian, will read the prayer or blessing before they go to bed. Then they return the piece of paper to the pocket and sleep on the pillow, thereby sleeping on the prayer or blessing.

Prayers may be sent from family or friends near or away. The learner may write a prayer or draw a picture about it, and then place it in their pocket of the Prayer Pillow. Instructions for the family should accompany the Prayer Pillow project. This activity may bring out discussion, moods, or feelings.

Other Intrapersonal Activities:

➢ Watch a video. Divide a sheet of paper into four pieces, and write down four things in the video that touch your heart or stand out for you.

➢ Write some statements or questions on individual pieces of paper. Fold the pieces of paper and put them in a jar. Invite a learner to pick a paper out of the jar, read what is written on the paper, and then share his or her personal opinion or viewpoint.

Examples of what to write on the pieces of paper:

How do you feel about prayer in public schools?

The most important thing a Sunday school leader can do for his or her learners is _____.

I love Jesus because_____.

If I could create something new in creation, it would be _____.

If the world is going to live in peace, we must _____.

➤ Read a story about Jesus. Talk about all the feelings represented in the story. Ask, "What do you think Jesus was feeling? What are you feeling as you read the story?" Invite the learners to write down their responses and then ask them to show what they wrote. See if any responses match.

BODILY/KINESTHETIC

Game Idea: Line Tag

Materials: masking tape, large open space, volunteers

Tape lines all over the floor of a large room or grassy area. Next, instruct the children that when their feet are on the lines, they have power—electricity—to move. They are to move all over the area, staying on the lines. They also can hop from line to line. If they step off the line, they must stop and get back on the line.

The game begins with one learner being "it." This learner must also stay on the lines as they chase the other learners. "It" tries to tag learners. When someone gets tagged, he or she is not "out," but receives a point instead. Volunteers help keep score and the goal is to have a score of zero.

"It" may not tag a learner two times in a row. Allow the game to be played for about two or three minutes before choosing another learner to be "it." To make the game even more fun, invite two or three people to be "it" at the same time. Caution the learners not to push and to be careful of collisions. After the game, talk about how God wants us to follow his "guideline" in life. Those guidelines are found in the 10 Commandments and through serving and loving others.

Other Bodily/Kinesthetic Activities:

➤ Teach a scripture verse for memory, but put music to it and add movements to enhance the learning.

➤ Play a part in a skit that teaches a Bible story. Have teams develop skits.

➤ Play charades or large-group drawing guessing game (similar to Pictionary) to relay a Bible story or a character.

➤ Use dance movements to portray a verse or story.

LOGICAL/MATHEMATICAL

Game Idea: Match It!

This game may be used for a Bible story review. The idea is to call out a person or an object from the Bible story, and then pick the matching theme, object, or person. Give two or three choices in matching. For example:

Name to call out	What is the match?
Adam and Eve	A. Camel B. Mustard seed C. Apple (correct)
The Prodigal Son	A. Father's inheritance (correct) B. A wedding C. A whale
Pentecost	A. Palm branches B. Wind and tongues of fire (correct) C. Old Testament

You may create more matches by what is being taught in your curriculum. Adapt the matches to age-appropriateness. This could be played with a team competition format.

Other Logical/Mathematical Activities:
➤ Put a long sheet of paper on the wall and draw a time line of the Bible.
➤ Make up a letter or number code to spell out a scripture passage.
➤ Categorize Bible story themes, finding stories in the Bible with a common theme such as children, animals, kings, or parables.

NATURALIST

Game Idea: Bible Scavenger Hunt
Use the outdoors to create a fun scavenger hunt. Relate the collected items to God's awesome creation.

An examples list of things to collect: bird feathers, a rock, a twig, a flower petal, some blades of grass, a pine cone.

Caution learners to be respectful of nature. They should only collect what has fallen on the earth's floor. After the items from nature have been collected, you may put together a nature collage combining several of God's creation themes.

Other Naturalist Activities:
➤ Take a boat ride and read a story from the Bible that has a boat in it.
➤ Lie under the stars and talk about how God created the whole universe.
➤ Grow a vegetable garden as a class. Celebrate a vegetable meal together. Also, share your garden profits!

Each of these games or activities may be embellished, added to, and changed to meet your individual curriculum needs. As Christian educators, we have a great opportunity to offer our learners the gift of teaching through a format that celebrates a multitude of learning styles. Games may be played in a wide variety of ways to enhance a learner's faith journey. Multiple intelligences celebrate the uniqueness of each individual learner.

We are called to teach a new way, to think differently as to how we share the good news with learners. We have a grand story to share. The story will live on. The future will be held through the storytellers. Live out the good news!

Questions and Answers

There are times when we are so excited to begin a new program or launch a pioneer project. I know what it is like to attend a conference or to read about a new ministry idea and be filled with enthusiasm to give it a try, and yet feel a bit reluctant because I'm just not sure how it will work in my setting.

I know that for some people, the use of games in Christian education may seem a bit odd at first, even uncomfortable. You may be questioning how the use of games will be effec-  tive in your Sunday school setting. You also may be wondering if active, experiential learning will be a comfortable teaching style for you.

Always allow questions and dialog to bubble up around newness and change. In order for any of us to teach with impact, we must feel confident and equipped as well as enthusiastic about all that we are about and doing. To educate is not to stuff in and force, but to draw out and encourage.

I worked with a leader who felt that incorporating games into her Sunday school class might cause her to lose control over the class. She was even worried that someone could possibly get hurt.

Our way through this was to first totally respect her voice, concerns, and commitment to teach Sunday school. Next, she and I spent time discussing active learning. Then, I modeled how to teach the Bible using games. And finally, I teamed her with another person who was well equipped in teaching the Bible using games. We were caring, respectful, and encouraging of that leader. She saw for herself through living out experientially how games had a most positive impact on children in teaching and sharing the gospel.

Following are a few questions and answers that may assist with your journey in weaving games into the tapestry of your curriculum.

*Question: **By implementing games, will we need to budget extra money into our Christian education curriculum costs?***

Answer: Games can be played with absolutely no equipment at all. All you need is an idea, a plan, a leader, and some kids! Beyond that, you could consider the benefits of adding materials, equipment, or resources to your Christian education curriculum, such as:

- ➢ utility balls
- ➢ beach balls
- ➢ a parachute
- ➢ sidewalk chalk
- ➢ equipment for an obstacle or ropes course
- ➢ game room
- ➢ a gym
- ➢ balloons
- ➢ feathers
- ➢ tumbling mats
- ➢ a whistle
- ➢ books, videos, tapes, or games about Christian education
- ➢ the expertise of a specialized game consultant (hired to come and train your leaders)

As you can see, you could be all over the board on supplies and equipment with what you purchase. Some Christian education leaders create a "wish list" of what they need, and the congregation is invited to donate items from the list. Be creative with your budget for games.

*Question: **Wait! I'm not a physical education teacher. How can I teach games?***

Answer: You don't have to be a physical education teacher, a coach, or a recreation specialist. But you do need training to ensure a quality experience for you and the learners. You're going to have to look upon training as a vital ingredient. In all areas of Christian education, we should always look upon training as important, expected, and ongoing.

Now, keep in mind that some people are naturally good at teaching games and active learning. They see the value of games in education and are very comfortable in teaching the total game process. Invite them to assist leaders and teach the teachers. Always be looking for resources. Gift each other by sharing your giftedness.

*Question: **Games often get learners revved up and rowdy. How will I guide them into a learning experience through games?***

Answer: I hear you—I've been there. Whenever I see that situation about to brew, I take great liberty to be very strict. Who is in control of the group—you or the learners? I realize some leaders are more comfortable with teaching and leading games than others.

I have stopped a game, reframed it, and begun again. I think that whenever learners are on the verge of being out of control, it is as though we are sending them across a high bridge with no railing—it is a frightening experience. The more you teach through the use of games, the more comfortable you will become with the whole process and the more you will develop a sense of a healthy control in multiple situations.

We know that some learners, when put in an active climate, can become over-stimulated. They may find it very difficult to settle into a discussion group. Be sensitive. Be caring. Shepherd that learner. Get to know your learners. Think proactively for them. But, in all situations, be strict—but do it in a way that they do not feel the environment is overly strict or unstimulating.

Question: ***How about those shy learners that prefer to be out on the fringe?***
Answer: Oh, yes, they are there. I've seen them and I've worked with them. I try to encourage them in a very loving way, but not to put an overly emphasized focus on them. I have asked other learners to be their buddy in working with them in a game.

I also think that it is perfectly fine for some learners to watch. They will learn—they will observe—they will glean the learning point in their own way.

I do move in enthusiastically when one learner doesn't want to play the game and thus several decide to do the same. The first step of the game teaching process is where we engage the learners. I step forth in encouraging everyone to be involved with the learning experience.

It's not always an easy journey. Just keep in mind: What would Jesus do in this situation? Or in any situation we encounter?

Also, keep in mind that some learners may hold back because that may not know many of the other learners. When they're with their friends, they maybe dive right in to an activity, but when they don't know others, they may hold back until they become familiar and comfortable with the people and the setting.

Question: ***What if a learner gets hurt during a game?***
Answer: A learner can get hurt walking into church or down a hallway or getting a drink from a water fountain. Kids fall, get bumps, scratches, and trip at times—just as we all do.

I suggest that you do all that you can to safeguard an experience during the preplanning process. Check through your plan. Look at the space. How is the equipment? Play out the game in your mind beforehand. Do your part in being responsible for a safe experience for all learners.

Also, do you have a first aid kit on hand? Are your leaders trained in first aid and CPR? I always make sure that I know who is current in their CPR training, where the first aid kit is (and that it is equipped), where the ice is, and that I have adult contact names and phone numbers for each learner. All Sunday schools should have this information.

I also feel that churches should have an accident form prepared and ready to use in the event of an injury. Always fill out the form and keep it on file. This goes for all ages and in all circumstances. Be proactive—not reactive.

Check through your plan. Look at the space. How is the equipment? Play out the game in your mind beforehand. Do your part in being responsible for a safe experience for all learners.

*Question: **How do I accommodate learners with special needs?***

Answer: I recently had a fifth grade girl, who was in a wheelchair, come to an evening of games in the gym for fourth, fifth, and sixth graders. We played line tag, dodge ball, and several fun games. She could use her arms to maneuver her wheelchair and did so as she moved into each game. I sensed that her arms were getting tired so I engaged several students to take turns pushing her during the games. She and all the students had a great time.

As leaders, we must look for creative ways to involve every learner in the whole Sunday school experience. I also enjoy involving the learners in finding ways to be inclusive. It is a part of the process of the game, and learners are very creative and have wonderful ideas as to how they can help.

There are many special needs to consider. In some cases, learners may require one or more helpers at their side to help them take part in active games. If a learner with a disability is eager to join his or her classmates and participate, we should do our very best to help make that participation a reality. Jesus welcomed all the children, and we need to do the same with all learners in our games.

Also, accommodating learners with disabilities in active games may be a teachable moment. As in the case of the girl above, the learners not only had fun playing games with each other, they also learned the value of service to each other. I imagine the girl in the wheelchair and those who assisted her may remember that evening for a long time to come. Impromptu opportunities of service can plant seeds of friendship, a pattern of greater service as Jesus teaches us to serve others, and maybe even influence future career paths.

A few examples of circumstances that present special needs you should consider are when learners:
- ➢ do not speak English
- ➢ are blind, deaf, or do not speak
- ➢ are limited in mobility
- ➢ are hyperactive or autistic
- ➢ are diabetic
- ➢ are on special medication
- ➢ have experienced a trauma in their lives, such as a death in the family, abusive touch, divorce, loss of a pet, a family move, change of school or church, loss of friendship, and so on

A leader will be better prepared if these issues are clearly addressed on a registration form. Include a section on your Sunday school registration form that asks about special needs or special concerns as well as any medication(s) a learner may be taking. This proactive step will help ensure a successful experience for the leader and, ultimately, the whole class.

And, of course, there are concerns and special needs that will not be written down on a registration form. When a learner is feeling sad, melancholic, frightened or confused, you have an "at the moment" experience to deal with. A learner may hide those feelings or display them on his or her face. Be sensitive to the emotional journey of a learner.

Leaders should find ways to accommodate learners with disabilities. However, if the learner doesn't want to participate, he or she should not be forced to do so.

Thoughts from the Front

Chapter 14

Why are games important for Christian education? Games:

G Greatly
A Advance a
M Multitude of
E Educational
S Situations

I talked with several people involved in Christian education in a variety of congregations—large and small. I asked them why they thought it was important to implement games in Christian education. Here are their thoughts.

From a Sunday School Leader

"Games are great! They get kids up, moving, and engaged! When we play games, kids always come up with things that are different than what I imagined, and they have wonderful ideas. Their creativity is astounding! Through games, you can spot kids that have real problem-solving skills and you also see kids become more aware of what other kids are feeling."

Deb Danielson
Sunday School Leader
White Bear Lake, Minnesota

From a Christian Educator

"The reason I think experiential learning is so important in Christian education is because we have the learners for such a limited amount of time. The message is crucial for their lives, and the only real way to have serious impact in so short a time is to use powerful teaching tools. Experiential learning has been proven to have much greater impact than static methods, so it only makes sense that we will want to do things the active way."

Vivian Rosquist
ELCA Partner in Education and Adjunct Staff
Christian Education
Montana Synod

From a Director of Preschool Ministry

"I think that when preschoolers interact with others, they learn more. Games help learners make connections—true connections. Through the learning experience of a game, learners will again and again revisit a thought, an idea, or something that they learned."

Sandy Cedergren
Director of Preschool Ministries
Mahtomedi, Minnesota

From a Camp Director

"In order to make the gospel real, we must provide varied opportunities for people of all ages and needs to experience the Word as alive. People learn best when they are involved in or experiencing the idea that is being learned. Well-chosen games can be used to foster Christian growth in a variety of ways to generate opportunities to reinforce God's message and to create shared experiences for people in Christian community.

"The youth group at First Lutheran Church, Portland, Maine, did a lock-in with the theme 'Faith, Grace, and Trust.' They began the evening with some games that made people laugh and move around. These games created a sense of trust and rapport within the group that facilitated the leader's approach to the evening's biblical theme.

"Later in the evening, the group divided into small groups. One person in each group was chosen as its leader. The others in the group were blindfolded. For the next half-hour, the leaders took their blindfolded teams through the church building—up stairs, down stairs, under pews, etc. At the end of the activity, the whole group got back together and talked about the experience. Discussion focused on communication, listening, worry, confidence, and trust. The youth leaders then shared some Bible verses and connected the blindfold activity with how Christians believe in Christ.

"Where does resistance to games come from? First it comes from the participants in the game. Group participants often have subtle or sometimes dramatic feelings of mistrust and find it difficult to play games. The person leading games may also harbor inner feelings of mistrust or low expectations to overcome in setting the stage for a good learning experience. Games are very effective with these issues.

"Sometimes resistance may come because games can produce noisy classes! Or maybe people are accustomed to having kids sit still and listen during Sunday school classes. It takes education of all in the congregation to understand the value of offering an active learning approach.

"An easy way to overcome these fears is to use educational theory regarding multiple intelligences to validate the use of games in Christian education. When people see how excited kids and adults are about hearing God's Word, the worries just disappear."

Miriam Englund
Camp Director for Family and Adult Programs
Calumet Lutheran Camp and Conference Center
New Hampshire

From a Pastor and Spiritual Director

"Games make learning fun. Games help us to loosen up on some of our heavy ideas about learning. Games can open up unique spaces for God to enter and show us new insights."

Lynn Pagliarini
Assistant Pastor of Worship and Spiritual Direction
Stillwater, Minnesota

From a Jamaican Sunday School Leader

"Using games and active learning is an absolute must. The children must live their learning. In teaching math, reading, language, and the Bible, the children learn through games, experiences, sounds, movement, music, and more. I have found this to be a most powerful way of teaching young children."

Juliet Brooks
Kindergarten Leader
Hope Valley Experimental School and Sunday School
Kingston, Jamaica, West Indies

From a School Volunteer Coordinator

"Games offer a hands-on experience. Using games offers a contemporary style of learning. When I was a child in Sunday school, I was told to sit still and listen. I did not participate. Now I see my children participate in Sunday school by involving many of their senses. Games help them bring the whole body into a learning experience. My children are enjoying their learning. Games are not passive, but rather an active learning process. Through games, there is more interaction with those around you. I think we grow to feel more comfortable with each other through games. In our school, we use a game process to help us in becoming responsive and respectful of each other. We find that we can teach values through games."

Kyra Ludwigson
Elementary School Volunteer Coordinator and
Small Group Leader in Women's Ministries
Pine Springs, Minnesota

From a Pastor of Education

"Games can break down barriers. The process of a game can help us get to know each other better and even help each other to relax. Games serve as great ice breakers. We can have fun and laugh through a game.

"I think that games are beneficial throughout all of our learning areas. Games help us reach across multiple generations. Games can appeal to the youngest, right on up to the oldest. I feel that games help to build community just as music does."

Duane Paetznick
Associate Pastor of Education
Apple Valley, Minnesota

From a Bible Study Facilitator

"Games help us to bring all our senses into a learning experience. Through a game, you may look, feel, smell, touch, hear—have a total body experience. Games help in getting everyone engaged. They assist in putting everyone on the same page of focus. Games involve movement. Games have a place in a multitude of learning areas. Everyone learns differently and games bring many of our senses into an experience.

"I'm always sensitive to the fact that not everyone enjoys a game, but I feel that the effort of implementing games in Christian education is worthwhile. In that we must be sensitive to others' needs, abilities, and comfort zones. Be ready to change a game by adapting it to make everyone feel included."

Kathy Warner
Camp Bible Study Leader and Facilitator
Dellwood, Minnesota

From a Director of Youth Ministries

"Games involve a variety of learning styles. Everyone learns in a different way. To really hit the mark and learning target, games are very useful. We can play a game to learn a theme. Games evoke relational ministry. We experience community, God, and each other through games. Games can have a profound effect on a group's desire to learn.

"We must be careful in implementing games. We may not assume that a game experience is comfortable for everyone."

Kyle Jackson
Director of Youth Ministries and Seminary Student
Hugo, Minnesota

From a Director of Children's and Family Ministries

"Games hit certain learning styles better than anything else. Games help us to remember key concepts. Games are a great way to evaluate what kids have learned."

Luanne Oklobzija
Director of Children's and Family Ministries
White Bear Lake, Minnesota

From a Director of Youth Ministry

"Outdoor ministry is experiential education, a hands-on active form of the gospel. This fact points to the effectiveness of experiential education. The Christian education ministry is a wonderful way of consistently reaching students of all ages with the gospel. The truth about experiential education is that it can—and should—be incorporated into the aspects of ministry that are already successful. It can enhance the ministry already occurring within a parish."

Jason Carrier
Lake Chautauqua Director of Youth Ministry
Upstate New York

Games help us to remember key concepts. Games are a great way to evaluate what kids have learned.

From an Outdoor Ministries Program Director

"Christianity and fun at the same time—what a revolutionary concept! Being a Christian should be a joyful experience, and kids see games as fun. So why not use games to teach the important lessons we have to share about faith? Games help campers relax, they bring the outsider in, encourage conversation, get the creative juices flowing, help us take a risk, and allow us to experience failure knowing we are still part of the group and still welcome. And games help younger campers develop their abstract learning skills. I've found that even the most simple game may open the door to a conversation with campers about rules, listening, friendships, responsibility, trust, love, forgiveness, serving, and so much more. Our system of using games and then debriefing is effective and appreciated by the churches we work with in the camp setting. It's informal education at its best and it's fun!"

Sunni Richardson
Associate in Ministry and Director/Programs
Nebraska Lutheran Outdoor Ministries

Ask those around you how they feel about the use of games in Christian education. Note their reactions and blend them with yours.

THE REAL GAME BEGINS

All right, here it is. You reading this resource—yes, you—the one who has said yes to proclaiming Christ to learners and their families. Yes, you—who plans, works, programs, checks out the latest resources, goes to conferences and training workshops, is leading people of all ages, works more hours that you are paid for, has a huge heart for teaching learners about Christ. You have said yes to a very high call, one of the highest calls that you will ever say yes to.

I'm ending this resource book by telling you that you are one of the richest, most valuable, treasured resources that your congregation will ever learn from. God has gifted and equipped you for this journey. In all of time, there will never be another one exactly like you—so, take good care of yourself. God is calling out to you, saying: You are mine, child, and I love you, I love you. You are a player and a coach in this game of living as a disciple.

Resources

Chapter 15

Bentley, William G., *Indoor and Outdoor Games* (Fearon Teaching Aids, 1966).

Bower, Nancy, *Adventure Play: Adventure Activities for Preschool and Early Elementary Children* (Project Adventure, 1998). Packed with games and activities to help very young learners begin to recognize concepts of cooperation, respect, and teamwork.

Cain, James and Barry Jolliff, *Teamwork and Team Play: A Guide to Cooperative, Challenge and Adventure Activities that Build Confidence, Cooperation, Teamwork, Creativity, Trust, Decision-making, Conflict Resolution, Resource Management, Communication, Effective Feedback and Problem-Solving Skills* (Kendall-Hunt Publishing Company, 1998).

Flinn, Lisa and Barbara Younger, *Making Scripture Stick: 52 Unforgettable Bible Verse Adventures for Children* (Group Publishing, Inc., 1992). Creative, hands-on learning techniques to bring Bible verses to life.

Fortier, Steve, Editor, *Youth Leadership in Action: A Guide to Cooperative Games and Group Activities* (Project Adventure, 1995). Written by and for youth leaders, it shares Project Adventure's best games, resources to develop strong youth leaders, and discussions on problems youth leaders may face and how to deal with them.

Glover, Donald R. and Daniel W. Midura, *Team-Building through Physical Challenges* (Human Kinetics Books, 1992).

Kotulak, Ronald, *Inside the Brain: Revolutionary Discoveries of How the Mind Works* (Andrews and McMeel, 1997). More than 300 brain researchers from around the world share how the brain works, which will help with planning activities.

Lingo, Susan L., *Instant Games for Children's Ministry* (Group Publishing Inc., 1995). Games using inexpensive, everyday items.

McCarthy, Bernice, *About Learning* (Excel, Inc., 1996). Explores how learning styles influence our lives.

Roehlkepartain, Jolene L., *101 Great Games for Kids: Active, Bible-Based Fun for Christian Education* (Abingdon Press, 2000). How to enthusiastically teach youngsters about faith and God's word.

Rohnke, Karl, *Silver Bullets: A Guide to Initiative Problems, Adventure Games, Stunts, and Trust Activities* (Project Adventure, Inc., 1984). A wide variety of creative indoor and outdoor activities to use in your camps.

Smith, Cindy, Ken Kellner, and Liz Shockey, *Helping Children Live Like Jesus: 3 Lessons from the Life of Christ* (Group Publishing, Inc., 1997). Complete sessions using Scripture, crafts, stories, object lessons, and more.

Youth Leadership in Action: A Guide to Cooperative Games and Group Activities (Kendall-Hunt Publishing Company, 1994). How youth leaders can implement experiential, cooperating activities and programs.

The following books are available at Augsburg Fortress Publishers by calling 1-800-328-4648.

Bickel, Kurt, *Funtastic Family Nights: 19 Family Night Programs* (Concordia Publishing House, 1998). Detailed instructions and event plans for offering fun family nights.

Davis, Kalisha, Compiling Editor, *Get Things Going: 50 Asset-Building Activities for Workshops, Presentations, and Meetings* (Search Institute, 2000). Lively asset-building activities that can be used in a wide variety of settings.

Everyone's a Winner: Games for Children's Ministry (Group Publishing, Inc., 1995). More than 100 games and activities to build cooperation in indoor and outdoor settings.

Kershner, Jan and Jody Brolsma, Editors, *Fun & Easy Games* (Group Publishing, Inc.,1998). Eighty-nine games where everyone finishes a winner!

Nilsen Family, *For Everything a Season: 75 Blessings for Daily Life* (Zion Publishing, 1999). Active blessings incorporating prayer, Scripture, reflections, and a ritual related to that blessing.

No-Miss Lessons for Pre-Teen Kids: 25 Faith-Building Lessons to Keep Kids Coming Back (Group Publishing, Inc., 1997) Complete, active-learning, attention-grabbing Sunday school sessions.

Roehlkepartain, Jolene L., *Building Assets Together: 135 Group Activities for Helping Youth Succeed* (Search Institute, 1997). Introducing developmental assets through creative, easy-to-use activities.

Augsburg Fortress Publishers
1-800-328-4648
www.augsburgfortress.org